Two Sides to Every Discussion

英語で考え、英語で発信する

Jonathan Lynch
Kotaro Shitori

音声ファイルのダウンロード／ストリーミング

CD マーク表示がある箇所は、音声を弊社 HP より無料でダウンロード／ストリーミングすることができます。トップページのバナーをクリックし、書籍検索してください。書籍詳細ページに音声ダウンロードアイコンがございますのでそちらから自習用音声としてご活用ください。

https://www.seibido.co.jp

Two Sides to Every Discussion

Copyright © 2015 by Jonathan Lynch, Kotaro Shitori

All rights reserved for Japan.
No part of this book may be reproduced in any form
without permission from Seibido Co., Ltd.

はじめに

　近年の英語教育では、従来の文法を重視した「読むこと」・「書くこと」に代わり、「聞くこと」・「話すこと」を主体とするコミュニケーションの重要性が声高に叫ばれています。これがはたしてどのような結果をもたらすことになるのか、確かなことは現時点では推測の域を出ません。ですが、ただひとつ明らかなことがあります。それは、よく言われていることですが、英語は世界の人々と意思疎通を図るための単なるツールに過ぎないということです。

　海外で生活すると切実に感じることでもありますが、他者に向けて自分の意見を表明することは、自分がどんな人間なのかを相手に深く理解してもらうための最も有効な手段であると同時に、自分の存在を認めてもらうために避けて通れないものでもあります。確かに、協調性が過度に重んじられる日本では、自分の意見を持つこと、そしてそれを主張することは、必ずしも周囲から好意的に受け入れられるとは限りません。それは多くの帰国子女の皆さんが実際に経験していることでもあります。ですが、こうした状況は世界的に見ても極めてまれであると言わざるを得ません。

　そうした意味でも、大切なのは近年の英語教育が目指している「英語が話せるようになること」ではなく、まずはその大前提として、「自分の意見をしっかり持つこと」なのです。ですから、「英語が話せるようになること」を一番の目標に設定する前に、まずは自分の内面とじっくり向き合って、人とは違うあなたらしい考えを持つことに意識の目を向けてください。それができるようになってから、英語というツールを使って発信できるように本格的に努力し始めても遅すぎることはありません。あなたが何者なのかを知ろうとする相手を前にして大事なことは、どう話すかではなく、何を話すかなのです。

　本テキストには、「教育」・「スポーツ」・「ライフスタイル」・「科学技術」・「食文化」・「ファッション」といった実に多岐にわたる分野から、皆さんにとって身近な話題が数多く取り上げられています。これらのテーマを前にしてあなたはどう考えるのか、ほかの人とは異なる独自の視点からひとつでも多くのユニークかつ説得力ある意見が出ることを、著者として楽しみにしています。

　最後になりましたが、本テキストの出版に際し、(株)成美堂編集部の菅野英一氏には大変御世話になりました。この場を借りて心より御礼申し上げます。有難うございました。

Jonathan Lynch
委文　光太郎

本書の使い方

Vocabulary in Context

　本文中で使用されている重要な単語や熟語が選び出されています。空欄に入るものを下の選択肢から選んでください。なお、わからない語句でも辞書は使わず、推測して答えてみましょう。

Reading

　まずは、辞書を使わずに本文をひと通り読んでみましょう。そしてそれが終わったら、今度は辞書を使用して、わからない単語や熟語の意味を調べながら何度もじっくりと読んでみましょう。最後に、CDを聞きながら音読することをおすすめします。

Note

　固有名詞や難しい語句の意味が説明されています。必要な時には参考にしてください。

Comprehension

　本文の内容が正確に理解されているかを確認するための質問です。該当する段落の番号を空欄に書き入れた上で、for または against のどちらかを○で囲んでください。

Grammar Point

　本文中で使用されている重要な文法事項が、簡潔に解説されています。本文を理解するための参考にしてください。

Writing

　自分の意見が英語で書けるようになるための練習です。参考になる例文が数多く提示されていますので、難しいと感じたときはそれらを参考にしてください。

Listening Dictation

　何の準備もなくいきなりCDを聞いて空欄を埋める方法も可能ですが、英文のおおよその意味を事前に理解したうえで音声を聞くことをおすすめします。問題が難しい場合は、先生に頼んでCDを何回も聞かせてもらいましょう。

Speaking

　毎回のテーマに基づいた会話モデルが提示されていますので、それを使用してクラスメートや先生にあなたの意見を伝えてみましょう。また、Writingで学習した表現もここで積極的に使用してみてください。

Column

　毎回のテーマについてさらに深く理解してもらうために、短いコラムが載せてあります。時間があれば、ぜひ読んでください。

CONTENTS

Part I Education and Sports

Unit 1 **University Entrance in Autumn** *1*
〈大学は秋入学にすべきである〉

Unit 2 **High School Sports Clubs** *6*
〈高校の部活は厳しすぎる〉

Unit 3 **Fingerprint Attendance System** *11*
〈授業の出欠には指紋認証を使うべきである〉

Unit 4 **Foreign Sports Players** *16*
〈プロスポーツにもっと外国人選手を使うべきである〉

Part II Lifestyle

Unit 5 **Experiences vs. Material Goods** *21*
〈物よりも経験を買う方が得である〉

Unit 6 **First Date** *26*
〈初デートは男性がお金を払うべきである〉

Unit 7 **Consumption Tax** *31*
〈消費税は15％に引き上げるべきである〉

Unit 8 **Female Pop Groups** *36*
〈女性アイドルグループは若い子に悪い影響を及ぼす〉

Part III Technology in Society

Unit 9 **Social Networking Services** *41*
〈SNSは有益なメディアである〉

Unit 10	Using Smartphones while Walking	46
	〈歩きスマホは違法にすべきである〉	
Unit 11	iPhone vs. Android	51
	〈iPhone は最高のスマートフォンである〉	
Unit 12	Video Gaming	56
	〈ゲームで遊ぶのは時間の無駄である〉	

Part IV Food and Culture

Unit 13	Celebrating Foreign Festivals	61
	〈外国のお祭りを祝うのは良いことである〉	
Unit 14	Eating on the Train	66
	〈電車内でものを食べても構わない〉	
Unit 15	Ramen	71
	〈ラーメンは体に良くないので食べないほうがよい〉	
Unit 16	Bread vs. Rice	76
	〈朝食はご飯よりもパンである〉	

Part V Appearance and Personality

Unit 17	Blood Types	81
	〈血液型で人の性格は正しく分類できる〉	
Unit 18	Cosmetic Surgery	86
	〈美容整形は良いことである〉	
Unit 19	Ear Piercing	91
	〈ピアスはするべきでない〉	
Unit 20	Wearing Perfume	96
	〈香水をつけるのは良いことである〉	

 University Entrance in Autumn

入学式といえば、桜が満開の春を思い出す人も多いでしょう。
ですが、日本のような4月入学は世界では少数派で、9月が主流です。
あなたはどちらが良いと思いますか。

Vocabulary in Context

次の下線部に入る語句を以下の語群から選んでください。

1. It is _____ to expect the university system to change quickly.
2. This freshman course will help to _____ your average TOEIC score.
3. English skills are _____ for students in this globalized world.
4. University students _____ study abroad if they have the chance.
5. This autumn, my club is going to _____ a performance for the school festival.
6. Finding a job is a(n) _____ challenge, but I will do my best.

> ought to   vital   raise   organize   huge   unrealistic

テーマ 大学は秋入学にすべきである

1. In Japan, the academic year starts in the spring. This is problematic and, in fact, should be changed.

2. Firstly, we must consider what is normal at universities in other countries. Data show that about 70 percent of universities around the world start their academic year in the autumn. Japan ought to change to the global standard.

3. Furthermore, because our schedule is different from foreign universities, it is difficult for Japanese university students to study abroad. If we synchronize our academic year with foreign countries, then Japanese students can more easily study at universities in other countries. Studying abroad is vital to help students gain a global outlook.

4. Finally, with this change, foreign students and researchers can more easily enter Japanese universities. More foreign people would internationalize our campuses and help to raise the quality of teaching and research.

5. Some people suggest that the Japanese academic year should start in autumn. This is not a good idea for the following reasons.

6. Firstly, we must consider the Japanese character. In Japan, people organize their lives according to the rhythm of the four seasons. Spring is the season for us to start new things. The appearance of the cherry blossoms, the fresh green leaves and the warm weather all help to motivate new students.

7. Autumn, on the other hand, is the first step towards the bleak winter. Leaves fall to the ground, flowers wither and the days grow colder and darker. It is hardly the best season for a bright start to university life.

8. In addition, changing to an autumn start for universities would cause huge disruption. It would mean that elementary schools, junior high schools and high schools would also have to change, and therefore the proposal is unrealistic.

Note

academic year 学年(度)　**problematic** 問題のある　**global standard** 国際標準　**synchronize A with B** AをBと一致させる　**outlook** 視野　**internationalize ~** ~を国際化する　**rhythm** リズム　**cherry blossom** 桜の花　**fresh green leaves** 新緑 (初夏の頃の若葉の緑)　**motivate ~** ~にやる気を起こさせる　**bleak** 寒々とした　**wither** 枯れる、しおれる　**disruption** 混乱　**elementary school** 小学校

Comprehension

次の文は本文の内容を要約したものです。該当する段落の番号を空欄に書き入れて、for または against のどちらかを○で囲んでください。

1	Autumn is not a suitable season to start the academic year.	7	for	(against)
2	It is easier for foreign students to study in Japan.		for	against
3	Japanese students can more easily study abroad.		for	against
4	It is best to make our system the same as systems in other countries.		for	against
5	Changing the start of the academic year would cause a lot of trouble.		for	against
6	Spring is the best time to start something new.		for	against

Grammar Point

不定詞の意味上の主語 : for + 名詞 + to do

1. ... it is difficult **for** Japanese university students **to** study abroad.
2. Spring is the season **for** us **to** start new things.

> 1. は「~が…すること」を意味する名詞用法で、2. は「~が…するための」を意味する形容詞用法である。この他に「~が…するように」を意味する副詞用法がある (例 を参照)。

例 The police officer stopped the car **for** the children **to** cross the street.

Writing

次の例文を参考にして、"**we must consider**…"の表現を学びましょう。

> この表現を使用することで、自分の意見を主張することができます。なお、considerの後には名詞 (**1.** を参照) や名詞節 (**2.** を参照) などがきます。

1. Firstly, **we must consider** the Japanese character.

2. Firstly, **we must consider** what is normal at universities in other countries.

さらに詳しく意見を主張したい時は、以下のように書くこともできます。

3. **We must consider** the global standard. Most countries have an autumn start.

それでは、下欄の for か against を○で囲んで、空欄を英語で埋めてみましょう。

```
I am  for / against  this proposal.

We must consider _____

_____

_____
```

Listening Dictation

CD を聞いて次の空欄を埋めましょう。

1. We must consider the Japanese climate. ¹⁾(　　　　) often ²⁾(　　　　) Japan in September, so it is not a good time to start school.

2. Japan ¹⁾(　　　　) has pleasant ²⁾(　　　　) in autumn, so it is a good time to start school.

3. I want to spend a year studying ¹⁾(　　　　), so I think it might be a good ²⁾(　　　　).

Speaking

次の会話モデルを使用して、クラスメートや先生にあなたの意見を伝えてみましょう。また、先ほど学習した表現も積極的に使用して下さい。

A Do you think the start of the university academic year should be moved to autumn?

B Yes, I think so.　OR　No, I don't think so.

A Why do you think that?

B [reason] _____

A OK. Anything else?

B Also, _____

_____

A I see.

B How about you? What do you think?

A I (also) think it should.　OR　I (also) don't think it should.

B Why do you say that?

A [reason] _____

　2012年に東京大学は秋入学への全面移行を目指しましたが、実施は当分見送るという結果になりました。ちなみに、あるデータによると日本の4月入学は世界的にもかなり珍しく、215カ国中、インドなどわずか7カ国だけのようです。

　そもそも日本はなぜ4月入学なのでしょうか。西洋から教育が導入された明治時代初期の入学時期は、実は9月でした。しかし、1886年に政府の会計年度が現在と同じ4月開始に変更されると、学事暦もそれに合わせることが望ましいと考えられるようになりました。さらに、同じ年の徴兵令改正によって、軍への入隊届出期限が9月から4月に早まると、師範学校に優秀な生徒が集まらないかもしれないと危惧する声が出てきました。こうした事態を避けるためにも、現在のような4月入学に徐々に移行していったと言われています。

UNIT 2 High School Sports Clubs

中学や高校時代の部活動がとても厳しかった、という人は少なくないでしょう。
その当時を振り返って、今あなたは部活動の在り方についてどう考えますか。

Vocabulary in Context

次の下線部に入る語を以下の語群から選んでください。

1. The *gymnasium is _____ for practice on Tuesdays and Thursdays
2. The baseball club coach has a(n) _____ as a tough but fair leader.
3. The summer training camp will _____ for six days.
4. The _____ training was worth it. We won the tournament!
5. Thanks to the advice of the coach and seniors, my _____ has improved.
6. The sumo club has no members, so the dohyo is never used. It's a(n) _____ .

*gymnasium：体育館

| reputation | available | waste | ability | severe | last |

高校の部活は厳しすぎる

1 Sports clubs at Japanese schools have a reputation for being very strict. In fact, they are too strict, for the following reasons.

2 Firstly, it is said that bullying occurs in many clubs. Some coaches bully and abuse the members. Some seniors bully the juniors. For example, my brother said that in his high school basketball club, juniors were sometimes punched or kicked by the seniors if they made a mistake. Such punishment is not necessary.

3 Secondly, not all students respond well to very strict conditions. Some students shine under a more nurturing approach. If only a strict approach is available, these kinds of students have no opportunity to do their best.

4 Finally, a strict approach may be reducing the sporting prowess of the club. Juniors waste a lot of time doing chores. If they spent that time practicing and developing their skills, the team could get better results.

5 It is easy to criticize school sports clubs in Japan as being too strict. However, this system is in fact very good for students.

6 Firstly, we must think about *gaman*. This is the Japanese word for endurance and is an important part of Japanese culture. We suffer and endure and thus reach new levels of ability. A strict sports club teaches us *gaman*, and that is a lesson that will help us in life.

7 Secondly, these days it is said that many young people are weak, both mentally and physically. They have been spoiled by their parents and society. They need to be toughened up and sports clubs do this. It may seem severe but they will certainly benefit.

8 Thirdly, the strict environment creates deep bonds among the members. Juniors have to help and encourage each other to survive the strict regime. The bonds this creates will last a lifetime.

UNIT 2

Note

sports club 運動部　**bullying** いじめ（動詞形はbully「～をいじめる」）　**nurturing approach** 才能を伸ばすやり方（指導法）　**sporting prowess** 優れた運動能力（prowessは「優れた能力」の意味）　**chore** 雑用　**be spoiled by ~** ～に甘やかされてだめにされる　**be toughened up** たくましく鍛えられる　**bond** きずな　**regime** 管理体制

Comprehension

次の文は本文の内容を要約したものです。該当する段落の番号を空欄に書き入れて、for または against のどちらかを○で囲んでください。

1	In a strict club, students can become tougher.		for	against
2	Students spend too much time doing chores and not enough time doing practice.		for	against
3	Deep friendships are formed in a strict club.		for	against
4	Students learn how to endure tough conditions in a strict club.		for	against
5	A strict atmosphere is not suitable for all students.		for	against
6	Bullying might be a problem in some clubs.		for	against

Grammar Point

部分否定 と 全否定

1. 部分否定：「すべてが～とはかぎらない」

   Secondly, **not all** students respond well to very strict conditions.

2. 全否定：「すべて～ではない」

   例 **None** of the students respond well to very strict conditions.

Writing

次の例文を参考にしながら、"**It is said that ~**"の表現を学びましょう。

   1. It is said that exercise is good for both mind and body.

   2. It is said that the coach is a tough but fair man.

また、同じような表現として次のようなものもあります。

   3. I have heard that ....

   4. My (friend / father / teacher / etc.) told me that ....

さらに、次の形を使用してあなた自身のケースについて話すこともできます。

   5. In my high school sports club, ...

それでは下欄のagreeかdisagreeを○で囲んで、その理由を英語で書いてみましょう。

I agree / disagree with this proposal.

Listening Dictation

CD 07

CDを聞いて次の空欄を埋めましょう。

1. It is said that a strict approach can be very 1)(   ) and even 2)(   ) for some students.

2. In a sports club, young people can 1)(   ) about discipline and how to 2)(   ) well.

3. Being a 1)(   ) of the volleyball club was one of my best 2)(   ) in high school.

UNIT 2

Speaking

次の会話モデルを使用して、クラスメートや先生にあなたの意見を伝えてみましょう。また、先ほど学習した表現も積極的に使用して下さい。

A Do you think that high school sports clubs are too strict?

B Yes, I think they are.   OR   No, I don't think they are.

A Why do you say that?

B [reason] _____

A OK. Any other reasons?

B Also, [reason] _____

A I see.

B How about you? What do you think?

A I (also) think they are too strict.   OR   I (also) think they are not too strict.

B OK. Please explain.

A [reason] _____

Column

　アメリカの学校の部活動はかなり日本とは異なるようです。日本では基本的に卒業するまで同じ部に所属しますが、アメリカでは春はバスケットボール、秋は野球というように、シーズンごとに競技そのものが替わります。また入部するには、「トライアウト」と呼ばれる厳しい試験をパスしなければなりません。そのため、バスケットボールやアメリカンフットボールといった人気スポーツは、初心者だと入部さえままならないとも言われています。ただその反面、日本のような上下関係の壁はなく、完全に実力主義であるため、力さえあれば1年生でも選手として対等に扱われるようです。
　どうやらアメリカの部活動には、良い点と悪い点がありそうですが、あなたはどちらの国の部活動に魅力を感じますか。

UNIT 3 Fingerprint Attendance System

大学を中心に、代返を防止するためのさまざまな取り組みが現在も行われています。もしあなたの学校で指紋認証の方式が取り入れられたら、どう思いますか。

Vocabulary in Context

次の下線部に入る語を以下の語群から選んでください。また必要に応じて語の形を変化させましょう。

1. I like the friendly _____ in our university.
2. I took the TOEIC test _____ times before I reached a score of 700.
3. The club members have _____ to keep the club room clean.
4. Our professor's classes are good because he tells us about _____ research in his field.
5. I wish my college _____ more native-speaker teachers of English.
6. Traveling abroad last year has _____ me to study English harder.

| current | encourage | responsibility | several | atmosphere | employ |

授業の出欠には指紋認証を使うべきである

1 Many universities have a problem with attendance. Unfortunately, some students cut class. Some teachers are strict about attendance, others are not. Also, the current methods used for roll call are time-consuming and it is easy to fake attendance. The whole system is a mess.

2 This could all be fixed by introducing a fingerprint sensor system.

3 Firstly, such a system would simplify things for both students and teachers. Students simply press their finger on the sensor at the start and end of a lesson and attendance is automatically recorded. Multiple sensors can be placed around big lecture halls.

4 Secondly, fake attendance would be reduced to zero. At present, it is not fair on the honest students when other students cheat the system.

5 Finally, fingerprint sensors would encourage students to take more responsibility for their own behavior. Instead of relying on the teacher, they themselves must ensure that their attendance is recorded.

6 A fingerprint sensor system for taking attendance cannot be recommended for university classes for a number of reasons.

7 The first of these is privacy. Having one's biometric data recorded several times a day would be an invasion of privacy. Our fingers are a part of our body and therefore giving a fingerprint is different from using a PIN number.

8 Secondly, universities have always been places of freedom and free thought. A fingerprint sensor system, on the other hand, would create an oppressive atmosphere, almost like a prison. We should avoid creating such an Orwellian environment, where "Big Brother" is watching us all the time.

9 The third reason is cost. A university-wide biometric system would be very expensive. That money could be better spent on employing more teachers or improving facilities. The existing systems may not be perfect but at least they are cost-effective.

Note

roll call 出席調べ（rollには「出席簿」の意味がある）　**time-consuming** 時間のかかる　**fake ~** ~を装う（形容詞形のfakeは「にせの、いんちきの」の意味）　**a mess** 収拾のつかない状態　**fingerprint sensor system** 指紋センターシステム　**big lecture hall** 大教室　**a number of ~** いくつかの~（「多くの~」という意味もある）　**biometric data** 生体情報　**PIN number** 暗証番号（PIN は personal identification number の略）　**Orwellian** オーウェル的な（英国の作家George Orwellが『1984』で描いた独裁主義体制の世界を指す）　**"Big Brother"** 「ビッグブラザー」（『1984』に登場する全体主義国家の独裁者。"Big Brother is watching you" と書かれたポスターが国中に貼られているが、その姿を見た者はいない）　**university-wide** 大学全体にわたる（wideが名詞の後に付いて「…全体の」という意味になる）　**cost-effective** 費用効果の高い、経済的な

Comprehension

次の文は本文の内容を要約したものです。該当する段落の番号を空欄に書き入れて、for または against のどちらかを○で囲んでください。

①	By using a fingerprint sensor system, we can stop people pretending to attend class.		for	against
②	A fingerprint sensor system would cost too much.		for	against
③	This kind of system would make taking attendance very simple.		for	against
④	Such a system seems too strict for a university.		for	against
⑤	Having to give your fingerprint data is an invasion of privacy.		for	against
⑥	A fingerprint sensor system would make students take more responsibility.		for	against

Grammar Point

some ~ others … :「~するものもいれば…するものもいる」

Some teachers are strict about attendance, ***others*** are not.

右の図のように、多数の「人」や「物」について、その中のいくつかをsomeで表し、残りの中のいくつかをothersで表す。

UNIT 3

Writing

次の2つの例文を参考にして、**would** の使い方を学習しましょう。

> **would**は「よく〜したものだ」（過去の習慣）や、「どうしても〜しようとした」（過去の意志）などを表しますが、**1.** と **2.** のように仮定法で使用されることも少なくありません。

1. It **would** be terrible if a war started over such a small thing.

2. A new computer system **would** make our jobs easier.
   (= If it were a new computer system, it would make our jobs easier.)

それでは下欄のagreeかdisagreeを○で囲んで、その理由を英語で書いてみましょう。

> I agree / disagree with this proposal.
> _____
> _____

Listening Dictation

CD を聞いて次の空欄を埋めましょう。

1. 1)(　　　　　) this system, students could check their 2)(　　　　　) online.

2. Fingerprint sensors are not 1)(　　　　　) and mistakes might often 2)(　　　　　).

3. My attendance is good 1)(　　　　　) any system would be 2)(　　　　　) with me.

Speaking

次の会話モデルを使用して、クラスメートや先生にあなたの意見を伝えてください。また、先ほど学習した would の表現も積極的に使いましょう。

A What do you think about using a fingerprint sensor system for attendance?

B I think it's a great idea.　OR　I don't think it is a good idea.

A OK. Why is that?

B [reason] _____

A I see. Anything else?

B [reason] _____

A That's interesting. I understand your position.

B How about you? What do you think?

A Well, I think it's a good idea (too).　OR　Well, I don't think it is a good idea (either).

B OK. Please explain.

A [reason] _____

　欠席した学生の出席を装うために他の学生が代わって返事をする「代返」は、今でも多くの大学関係者を悩ませています。近年では、テクノロジーの進化により、ICカード付き学生証やスマートフォンなどを使って出席を管理する大学が増えていますが、問題はなかなか解決していないようです。

　一方海外の大学では、授業の前に毎回大量の本を読まなければならなかったり、授業中にたくさん発言することが求められたり、レポートが数多く出されたり、試験が難しかったりというように、単位の取得そのものに大変な困難が伴うため、授業に出るのは当たり前というのが実情のようです。

　いつの日か、日本でも代返という言葉そのものがなくなることを願わずにはいられません。

UNIT 4 Foreign Sports Players

スポーツ観戦が趣味の人はたくさんいると思いますが、
あなたは今よりも多くの外国人選手にプレーして欲しいですか。
それとも、もっとたくさんの日本人選手が試合に出ることを望みますか。

Vocabulary in Context

次の下線部に入る語を以下の語群から選んでください。また必要に応じて語の形を変化させましょう。

1. The _____ of soccer in Japan is improving year by year.

2. A(n) _____ speaker of English is someone who speaks English as his or her first language.

3. The _____ to change the school baseball team's uniform was not popular.

4. Joining a sports team is a(n) _____ way to make friends.

5. High school baseball teams in Japan _____ in the annual "Koshien" tournament.

6. Our school soccer team _____ the final of the *prefectural tournament last year.

*prefectural tournament：県大会

| standard   excellent   reach   proposal   native   compete |

プロスポーツにもっと外国人選手を使うべきである

For

1 Recently, attendance at professional baseball and soccer games in Japan has been stagnant. We need to revitalize these sports and the best way is to allow more foreign players to play in Japan's professional leagues.

2 The first point in favor of this is excitement. Foreign players add unpredictability to matches, which makes them more exciting to watch. If there were more foreign players, then the matches would be more exciting.

3 The second point is money. More foreign players could lead to higher attendance and therefore more revenue for clubs. Also, Japanese leagues would become more interesting for other countries to watch on TV and this would increase advertising revenues.

4 Thirdly, we have to raise the level of Japanese sports to international standards. Having mainly Japanese players means that there is the risk of a "Galapagos effect." Excellent foreign players can help Japanese players reach new levels of ability.

Against

5 In theory, it may seem to be a good idea to have more foreign athletes in Japanese professional leagues. In practice, however, this proposal cannot be recommended. There are several reasons.

6 Firstly, if more foreign players came, the opportunities for Japanese athletes would decrease. There would be fewer places in teams for native Japanese players, and fewer young people would have the chance of a career in sports.

7 Secondly, surely it is better for young Japanese players to reach international level by going abroad and playing in a foreign league. In fact, such players get a lot of TV coverage in Japan, which means that Japanese fans can enjoy seeing both foreign players and Japanese players competing together.

8 Finally, bringing foreign players to Japan can be very expensive. Only wealthy teams might be able to buy a lot of foreign players and, if they did so, the leagues would become unbalanced.

UNIT 4

> **Note**
> **attendance** 観客数　**stagnant** 低迷した　**revitalize ~** ~を活性化させる　**professional league** プロリーグ　**unpredictability** 予測不能性　**advertising revenue** 広告収入　"**Galapagos effect**"「ガラパゴス化」(「ガラケー」と呼ばれる日本の携帯電話のように、国内で独自の発展を遂げて国際標準からかけ離れてしまうこと)　**TV coverage** テレビ放送

Comprehension

次の文は本文の内容を要約したものです。該当する段落の番号を空欄に書き入れて、for または against のどちらかを○で囲んでください。

1	Having more foreign players means fewer opportunities for Japanese players to play.		for	against
2	Clubs can make more money if more foreign players are used.		for	against
3	It is better for Japanese players to get experience in foreign leagues.		for	against
4	Foreign players make matches more exciting.		for	against
5	If Japanese players are mainly used, ability levels will not change.		for	against
6	It is too expensive to bring a lot of foreign players to Japan.		for	against

Grammar Point

関係代名詞 which の非制限用法（継続用法）

1. *Foreign players add unpredictability to matches,* **which** *makes them more exciting to watch.*
2. *In fact, such players get a lot of TV coverage in Japan,* **which** *means that Japanese fans can enjoy seeing both foreign players and Japanese players competing together.*

> 非制限用法は先行詞を補足的に説明するもので、関係代名詞の前にコンマが置かれる。また、**1.** と **2.** の文のように、非制限用法のwhichに限り、前の節全体またはその一部を先行詞とすることができる。

Writing

次の例文を参考にしながら、仮定法を使った表現を学習しましょう。

> 本文中では、すべて仮定法過去が使用されています。仮定法過去は、「現在の事実と反対の仮定」（**1.** と**2.** 参照）と「現実に起こる可能性が乏しい未来のことについての仮定」（**3.** を参照）を表します。本文では、主に「外国人選手が少ない」という現在の事実と反対の仮定（「もし外国人選手がもっと多ければ」）として、仮定法過去が使用されています。

> 仮定法過去：「もし〜なら、…だろうに」
> If + S + 動詞の過去形, S + would (couldなど) + 動詞の原形

1. **If** there **were** more foreign players, then the leagues **would** be more exciting.
2. **If** there **were** too many foreign players, young people **would** have fewer opportunities.
3. **If** I **won** the lottery, I **would** buy a Ferrari sports car.

それでは下欄の for か against を○で囲んで、どちらか一方を英語で埋めてみましょう。

> I am for / against   this proposal.
>
> FOR : If there were more foreign players, _____
>
> AGAINST : If there were more/too many foreign players, _____
>
> _____

Listening Dictation

CDを聞いて次の空欄を埋めましょう。

1. If there were more ¹⁾(   ) players, it would make our leagues more ²⁾(   ) and interesting.

2. We can see ¹⁾(   ) ²⁾(   ) foreign players on satellite TV or ³⁾(   ) the World Cup.

3. ¹⁾(   ) more players from other ²⁾(   ) countries might be a good idea.

Speaking

次の会話モデルを使用して、クラスメートや先生にあなたの意見を伝えてみましょう。また、先ほど学習した表現も積極的に使用して下さい。

A Do you think that more foreign players should play in Japan's professional leagues?

B That's a good question! Well,　yes, I do.　OR　no, I don't.

A OK. Why do you say that?

B [reason] _____

A Anything else?

B Yes. [reason] _____

A Thanks for explaining your opinion.

B How about you? What do you think?

A Well,　I think it is a good idea (too).　OR　I don't think it's a good idea (either).

B Why's that?

A [reason] _____

　　日本の多くのプロスポーツリーグには、プレーする外国人選手の出場枠を意味する、いわゆる「外国人枠」というものが存在します。中でもよく知られているのが、野球とサッカーのリーグかもしれません。

　　日本のプロ野球では、1軍の出場選手登録は4人までとなっています（ただし、投手と野手はそれぞれ最大3人までしか登録できません）。またサッカーのJリーグ1部では、3人の外国人選手に、アジア枠（またはタイなどのJリーグ提携国枠）の1人を加えた最大4人の出場登録が可能です。

　　ちなみに、海外出身の力士がたくさんいるように思える大相撲の世界にも、「外国出身力士は各相撲部屋に1人まで」というルールがあるそうです。皆さんは知っていましたか？

Experiences vs. Material Goods

「最近の若者は消費しない」と言われることがありますが、あなたは買い物と旅行だったらどちらにお金を使いますか。

Vocabulary in Context

次の下線部に入る語を以下の語群から選んでください。また必要に応じて語の形を変化させましょう。

1. I bought a(n) _____ new item the other day. It's a *selfie stick!
2. Buying cheap things is not a good _____. They soon break.
3. My spending money comes _____ from my part time job.
4. I _____ to go abroad and see all the famous places with my own eyes.
5. Traveling _____ many opportunities to have fun and learn new things.
6. Even bad _____ can teach us many things.

*selfie stick：自撮り棒

| yearn | mainly | experience | interesting | provide | investment |

物よりも経験を買う方が得である

❶ Many young people yearn to buy things such as electronic gadgets, clothes, accessories and so on.

❷ The truth is that buying these items will not make them happy. Instead, they would be better off by using their money mainly for experiencing things such as traveling to a new place or participating in an activity.

❸ Firstly, experiences give us deep memories that stick with us all our lives. This cannot be said about mere objects which will be forgotten as soon as they become obsolete or broken.

❹ Secondly, experiences develop us and help us to grow as human beings. We learn more about the world and about ourselves with every new thing we try and every new place we visit.

❺ And one more important point is that experiences make us more interesting people. Someone who has been to many places and done many things has a lot of interesting stories to tell.

❻ Spending money mainly on experiences rather than buying things sounds nice in theory, but in the real world it is not that simple.

❼ For a start, buying things is good. Indeed, this activity forms the basis of our capitalist economic system. It provides many people with jobs—not just manufacturers, but also people involved in distributing, marketing and selling goods.

❽ Secondly, shopping for new things is enjoyable. Who can deny the excitement of buying something new, bringing it home and using it or wearing it for the first time? That thrill is a natural feeling for humans, especially if we have worked hard to pay for the item.

❾ And thirdly, whereas an experience is over in minutes, hours or days, a much-loved item keeps on giving pleasure for months or years. Therefore, buying something you really want gives a good return on your investment.

Note

electronic gadget 電子機器 **The truth is that ~** 実を言うと～ **be better off** より幸せになる (原級はwell off) **stick with ~** ～(の頭) から離れない (stickは「くっつく」の意味) **obsolete** 旧式の、流行遅れの **that** そんなに、それほど (日常会話の中で副詞的に使用される) **for a start** まず第一に、そもそも (= to start with) **capitalist economic system** 資本主義経済システム **manufacturer** 製造業者 **distributing** 流通、配達 **whereas ~** ～であるのに対して **much-loved** 大好きな **return** 見返り

Comprehension

次の文は本文の内容を要約したものです。該当する段落の番号を空欄に書き入れて、for または against のどちらかを○で囲んでください。

			for / against
①	Experiencing many things makes great memories.		for / against
②	Shopping is fun.		for / against
③	Because we can use an item for a long time, we can gain a lot of satisfaction from it.		for / against
④	Purchasing goods helps the economy.		for / against
⑤	The more we experience, the more we develop ourselves.		for / against
⑥	Hearing stories from someone who has experienced many things is very interesting.		for / against

Grammar Point

something + 形容詞

*Who can deny the excitement of buying **something new**...*

some, any, no, every に -thing, -one, -body をつけた代名詞に形容詞がつく場合、形容詞は後に置かれる。

例 1. The doctor says there is **nothing wrong** with me.

例 2. I have never met **anyone stronger** than you.

例 3. My Twitter account was used by **somebody unknown**.

UNIT 5

Writing

2つの例文を参考にしながら、次の表現を学びましょう。

> … **sounds** ＋形容詞＋ **but in fact** …

1. University **sounds** enjoyable **but in fact** there is a lot of hard studying.
2. Professor Martin's course **sounds** easy **but in fact** it is hard to get a good grade.

それでは、下欄の FOR か AGAINST のどちらかを選んで空白部分を英語で埋めてください。

FOR :   Using money to buy many items sounds ＿＿＿＿＿ but in fact

＿＿＿＿＿＿＿＿＿＿＿＿＿＿＿＿＿＿＿＿＿＿＿＿＿＿＿＿＿＿＿＿

AGAINST :   Using money for experiences sounds ＿＿＿＿＿ but in fact

＿＿＿＿＿＿＿＿＿＿＿＿＿＿＿＿＿＿＿＿＿＿＿＿＿＿＿＿＿＿＿＿

Listening Dictation

 16

CD を聞いて次の空欄を埋めましょう。

1. Travel abroad sounds 1)(　　　　) but in fact a trip is soon finished. Buying something 2)(　　　　) such as a tablet gives benefits over a long period.

2. By 1)(　　　　) things such as travel and new activities, we can make lots of 2)(　　　　).

3. I 1)(　　　　) I had enough money to 2)(　　　　) experience many things and do a lot of shopping!

Speaking

次の会話モデルを使用して、クラスメートや先生にあなたの意見を伝えてください。また、先ほど学習した表現も積極的に使いましょう。

A Which do you think is better, experiencing things or buying things?

B Well, I think _____ is better.

A OK. Why do you say that?

B [reason] _____

A I see. Anything else?

B Another point is _____
_____

A That's interesting.

B How about you? What do you think?

A I agree with you. *OR* I think [reason] _____
is better.

B OK. Please explain.

A Sure. [reason] _____

　　幸福度の上がるお金の使い方について、アメリカの大学のある心理学者が調査したところによると、貴金属やバッグといった物を買うよりも、旅行やコンサートなどにお金を使う方が、より大きな幸福が得られるという結果が出たそうです。また別の調査では、「人は買ったものについて話すことよりも、お金を使った経験について話すことを好む」というデータもあるようです。

　ですが、例えば一生懸命働いたお金でずっと欲しかった腕時計を購入すれば、その腕時計を見るたびに、頑張って働いた過去の記憶がよみがえるかもしれません。そして、その記憶がその人の自信につながることは十分考えられることです。はたして、物と経験どちらが私たちをより幸せにしてくれるのでしょうか。

UNIT 6 First Date

最初のデートは男性が支払うのか、それとも割り勘にするのか。
あなたは、男性としてまたは女性として、どちら派ですか。

Vocabulary in Context

次の下線部に入る語句を以下の語群から選んでください。また必要に応じて語の形を変化させましょう。

1. Valentine's Day is the perfect _____ to ask someone for a date.

2. David is very _____ . He often buys presents for his girlfriend.

3. I don't want to _____ my boyfriend like a mother. He should be strong and independent.

4. Checking mail on your smartphone is _____ on a first date.

5. He didn't make a good _____ . He just talked about himself all evening.

6. On the first date, dress up! And that _____ both women and men.

| generous   impression   look after   apply to   opportunity   unacceptable |

初デートは男性がお金を払うべきである

1 These days society is aiming for equality between the sexes. That is obviously a good thing but there is one thing that should not change—men paying on the first date.

2 The first point to support this is chivalry. Even today, men should make an effort to behave like gentlemen. Part of this is being generous and kind. A first date is the perfect opportunity for a man to show his gentlemanly character by paying for everything.

3 The second point is that men must avoid being mean. No woman likes a stingy guy and, frankly speaking, asking to split the bill on the first date gives that impression.

4 Finally, it may be outdated, but men have a natural urge to protect and look after women. If only for the first date, a man should be his true self and fulfill that role. Equality can start from the second date.

5 Now is the time for society to change. The keyword is equality and this also applies to dating.

6 Firstly, it is unfair for women to expect equal opportunities in society, but yet also to expect men to pay on the first date. That is a double standard and unacceptable.

7 The second point is that, these days, women should avoid being submissive to men. If the man pays for the first date, he already seems to be in a more powerful position in the relationship. The woman seems to be just meekly accepting his favor. That is not good.

8 The third point is that the man is also judging the woman on a first date. If she expects everything to be paid for, then the guy may think she is either poor or stingy, or both poor and stingy. She should offer to pay half.

UNIT 6

Note

chivalry 騎士道精神（勇気・忠誠などをモットーとし、女性を敬い弱者を助けるといった資質）　**mean** けちな（stingyも同じ意味）　**frankly speaking** 率直に言えば　**split the bill** 割り勘にする　**outdated** 時代遅れの　**if only for ~** ～だけでも（if には even if のような「たとえ～でも」という譲歩の意味がある）　**equal opportunity** 機会均等　**but yet** それにもかかわらず、それでいて一方では　**double standard** 二重基準（対象によって異なる価値判断の基準を使い分けること）　**submissive** 従順な　**meekly** おとなしく、従順に

Comprehension

次の文は本文の内容を要約したものです。該当する段落の番号を空欄に書き入れて、for または against のどちらかを○で囲んでください。

1. It is strange for women to expect equality but also to expect men to pay on a date. —— for / against
2. Men should not be stingy. —— for / against
3. It is natural for men to take care of women. —— for / against
4. Men also judge women on the first date. —— for / against
5. Gentlemanly behavior is still important. —— for / against
6. Women should aim to be equal to men on the first date. —— for / against

Grammar Point

動名詞 のさまざまな働き

1. 補語になる　*Part of this is **being** generous and kind.*
2. 目的語になる　*The second point is that men must avoid **being** mean.*
　　　　　　　*... women should avoid **being** submissive to men.*
3. 主語になる　*... **asking** to split the bill on the first date gives that impression.*
4. 動名詞の意味上の主語を示す必要がある場合は、動名詞の前に置く
　　*... but there is one thing that should not change—**men paying** on the first date.*

Writing

次の **3** つの例文を参考にして、**should** の使い方を学習しましょう。

> **should** は「〜するほうがよい」という弱い義務や勧告を表します。強く言いたい場合は**must**を使いましょう。

1. If .... then men **should** pay for everything. / women **should** pay half.

2. Men **should** pay for everything because ....
   Couples **should** split the bill because ....

3. Men .... so they **should** pay for everything.
   Women .... so couples **should** split the bill.

それでは、agree か disagree を○で囲んでその理由を英語で書いてみましょう。

```
I am  for / against   this proposal.
_____
_____
```

Listening Dictation

CD 19

CD を聞いて次の空欄を埋めましょう。

1. On １⁾(   ) , men ²⁾(   ) more money than women, so they should pay.

2. ¹⁾(   ) days, women can earn ²⁾(   ) ³⁾(   ) money as men, so couples should split the bill.

3. I've never ¹⁾(   ) on a date, so this topic is ²⁾(   ) for me to imagine.

UNIT 6

Speaking

次の会話モデルを使用して、クラスメートや先生にあなたの意見を伝えてください。また、先ほど学習した表現も積極的に使いましょう。

A Do you think that men should pay for everything on the first date?

B Tricky question, but…　yes, I do.　*OR*　no, I don't.

A Why is that?

B [reason] _____

A I see. Anything else?

B Also, [reason] _____

A That's interesting.

B How about you? Do you think men should pay?

A Yes, I do.　*OR*　No, I don't.

B OK. Please explain.

A [reason] _____

　　20代から30代の日本人を対象としたある意識調査で、「初デートの支払いはどうするか」と聞いたところ、男性は「男性が全額もしくは多めに払う」が約80％で、「割り勘にする」が約15％でした。一方、女性側の回答は「男性が全額もしくは多めに払う」が約60％で、「割り勘にする」が約30％という結果でした。

　　ちなみに海外では、「デートの支払いは絶対に男性」という国が最も多いようで、中でもイタリア人男性は、破産してでも必ず支払うと言われているそうです（真偽の程は定かではありません）。

Consumption Tax

2014年に消費税が引き上げられましたが、世界的に見れば日本の税率はまだまだ低いと言われています。あなたはさらなる消費税の引き上げに賛成ですか。それとも反対ですか。

Vocabulary in Context

次の下線部に入る語を以下の語群から選んでください。また必要に応じて語の形を変化させましょう。

1. The Japanese "bubble economy" _____ in 1991.
2. These days, there is a(n) _____ gap between rich and poor people.
3. The unemployment _____ in Japan is about four percent.
4. I _____ some money from everybody to buy Susan a birthday present.
5. You can earn some _____ money by working overtime.
6. International sporting events can _____ big profits for Japanese companies.

| rate | huge | collect | collapse | generate | extra |

消費税は15％に引き上げるべきである

❶ Recently in Japan, consumption tax has been raised incrementally. While this policy is correct, it is not enough. In fact, the rate of consumption tax should be increased to 15 percent.

❷ Firstly, the number of elderly people in Japan is increasing, and the costs of health care and pensions will skyrocket from now on. The only way to cover these huge costs is through a higher consumption tax.

❸ Secondly, even a 10 percent consumption tax is very low in international terms. In Germany, for example, VAT is about 19 percent. Surely our current rate of consumption tax is abnormally low in comparison.

❹ Finally, consumption tax is a good tax to increase because it is fair and simple. Rich people buy more luxury goods, so they pay more tax. Also, for shops and other businesses, it is a very simple tax to collect and pay to the government.

❺ The proposal to increase consumption tax to 15 percent must be rejected for a number of reasons.

❻ First of all, such a big increase would have a negative effect on the economy. People would buy fewer goods and so manufacturers would have big problems. The service industry would suffer too. In fact, it could lead to an economic collapse.

❼ The second point is that, although the proposal would generate more tax revenue, that extra revenue might not be used appropriately. Governments would probably use it on projects which benefit themselves and their supporters, not for covering the costs of social services.

❽ Thirdly, consumption tax cannot be considered a fair tax. If somebody buys a loaf of bread, they pay the same tax, regardless of whether they are rich or poor. That can hardly be called fair. If a tax increase is necessary, an income tax increase would be fairer.

Note

consumption tax 消費税　**incrementally** 徐々に　**pension** 年金　**skyrocket** 急激に上昇する　**in international terms** 国際的に見ると (in … termsは「～の点から」の意味)　**VAT** 付加価値税 (value-added taxの略語、日本の消費税に相当する)　**service industry** サービス (産) 業 (運輸・通信・金融などサービスを提供する産業の総称)　**tax revenue** 税収 (revenueは「歳入、収入」の意味)　**social services** 社会福祉事業　**a loaf of bread** パン一個 (loafは「パンの一塊」の意味)　**income tax** 所得税

Comprehension

次の文は本文の内容を要約したものです。該当する段落の番号を空欄に書き入れて、for または against のどちらかを○で囲んでください。

①	By international standards, Japan's consumption tax rate is very low.		for	against
②	More tax revenue is needed to help care for elderly people.		for	against
③	Consumption tax is an unfair tax.		for	against
④	Raising consumption tax will have a negative effect on the economy.		for	against
⑤	Consumption tax is fair and easy to collect.		for	against
⑥	Revenue from consumption tax might be used inappropriately.		for	against

Grammar Point

so that

1. 目的：「〜するため(よう)に」

   ● so that の前には通例コンマを置かない。口語ではthatが省略されることがある。

   例 The teacher spoke loudly **so (that)** everyone could hear her.

2. 結果：「それで、その結果」

   ● so that の前にコンマを置くことが多い。口語ではthatが省略されることがある。

   Rich people buy more luxury goods, **so (that)** *they pay more tax.*

Writing

次の 2 つの例文を参考にして、**because** と **and so** の使い方を学習しましょう。

1. の例文のように「理由」を強調したい場合に、because が使用されます。

1. Everybody is complaining **because** taxes increased last month.

2. Taxes increased last month **and so** everybody is complaining.

それでは下欄の for か against を○で囲み、どちらか一方にその理由を英語で書いてください。

I am for / against   this proposal.

1. Raising consumption tax is (good / bad) because _____

_____

2. _____

and so raising consumption tax is (good/bad).

Listening Dictation

 22

CD を聞いて次の空欄を埋めましょう。

1. Raising consumption tax could be 1)(　　　　) for everybody because social services would 2)(　　　　) .

2. I already 1)(　　　　) a lot of tax and so I think consumption tax should 2)(　　　　) 3)(　　　　) increased.

3. At some shops in Japan, tourists from 1)(　　　　) do not 2)(　　　　) 3)(　　　　) pay consumption tax.

Speaking

次の会話モデルを使用して、クラスメートや先生にあなたの意見を伝えてください。また、先ほど学習した表現も積極的に使いましょう。

A Do you think it is a good idea to raise the consumption tax to 15 percent?

B Yes, I do.   OR   No, I don't.

A OK. Please explain why.

B [reason] _____

A I see. Anything else?

B [reason] _____

A Thanks for telling me.

B How about you? What do you think?

A I (also) think that it's a (good/bad) idea.

B OK. Could you explain?

A [reason] _____

　　本文にも書かれていたように、海外と比較すると日本の消費税は依然としてかなり低いと言えるでしょう。ですが問題は、単に高いか低いかということではないのかもしれません。

　　例えばスウェーデンを見てみましょう。この国の消費税率は現在25％で、日本よりもはるかに高い税率です。しかし、スウェーデンは軽減税率を設けているため、例えば公共交通機関は6％、食料品は12％に抑えられています。さらに、19歳未満は医療費が無料で、大学までは教育費もかかりません。

　　このように、一見すると25％というのは異常な数字に見えますが、何より重要なのは、国民が支払った税金がきちんと国民のために活用されているのかどうかということかもしれません。

UNIT 8 Female Pop Groups

大人数からなる女性アイドルグループが最近人気を集めていますが、好き嫌いの問題はさておき、あなたはこの現象についてどう思いますか。

Vocabulary in Context

次の下線部に入る語を以下の語群から選んでください。また必要に応じて語の形を変化させましょう。

1. The _____ reason for her popularity is her cute appearance.
2. Successful female singers are _____ role models for young girls.
3. My music teacher was the _____ for my career as a musician.
4. After _____ from university, I want to become a rock star!
5. In the music business, success _____ fame and fortune.
6. The media sometimes _____ a negative image of rap and hip-hop music.

| promote | main | graduation | positive | inspiration | bring |

女性アイドルグループは若い子に悪い影響を及ぼす

For

[1] Wherever we look these days, it seems that female pop groups with large numbers of members appear. While they may be popular, they are in fact a negative trend for young girls.

[2] Firstly, these groups promote the stereotype that the main role for females is to be cute. The message seems to be that, as long as girls look cute and act cute, it is enough... nothing more is expected.

[3] Secondly, the truth is that, behind the scenes, these groups are controlled by men. These men decide everything and also take most of the money. In a way, the group members seem to be just puppets for men.

[4] Furthermore, these groups have a system of "graduation." In fact, this is just a euphemism for firing people. It is reminiscent of *kata tataki*, the old system used by companies to fire women when they reached 25. Surely these pop groups are taking women backwards, not forwards.

Against

[5] In recent years, a popular new type of group has appeared. Each group has a large number of female members and their catchy songs are enjoyed by both men and women. More than that, these groups are a positive trend for young girls for the following reasons.

[6] First of all, these groups show girls that there are many opportunities in life. They help to motivate girls to go out into society and find success. Through their members' success, they provide inspiration for girls.

[7] Secondly, it is not easy to become members of such groups. All the members have worked very hard to develop their cute style and dancing ability. In this way, the groups show young girls that hard work brings results.

[8] Finally, these groups serve as a springboard from which the members can launch a career in show business. Ex-members may become successful as solo artists or even as actresses.

UNIT 8

> **Note**
>
> **stereotype** 固定観念　**behind the scenes** 舞台裏で、陰で　**in a way** ある意味では　**puppet** 操り人形　**euphemism for ~** ～の遠回しな言い方、婉曲語　**be reminiscent of ~** ～を思い出させる　**catchy** 覚えやすい　**go out into ~** ～に出る（= enter）　**springboard** 踏み台　**show business** 芸能界、ショービジネス　**ex-member** 元メンバー

Comprehension

次の文は本文の内容を要約したものです。該当する段落の番号を空欄に書き入れて、for または against のどちらかを○で囲んでください。

			for / against
1	The members of these pop groups can have successful careers after leaving the group.		for / against
2	It is good for young girls to see that the group members are working very hard.		for / against
3	The members just seem to have a cute appearance and nothing else.		for / against
4	"Graduation" from the group actually means being fired.		for / against
5	The success of these groups is inspiring for young girls.		for / against
6	These pop groups are completely controlled by men.		for / against

Grammar Point

前置詞 ＋ 関係代名詞

*Finally, these groups serve as a springboard **from which** the members can launch a career in show business.*

> 以下のように、先行詞は a springboard で、which は直前の前置詞 from の目的語の働きをしている。

*These groups serve as **a springboard**.　The members can launch a career in show business from **it**.*

which

Writing

次の例文を参考にして、反論する表現を学習しましょう。

> It is said that the members of these groups have cute faces and nothing else. **In my opinion, that is not true.** They can dance and sing. They are great entertainers.

それでは賛成か反対の立場を決めて、先ほどの表現を使用しながら、英語で反論してみましょう。

I am for this proposal. It is said that many members of these groups become successful after they leave. In my opinion, that is not true. _____

I am against this proposal. It is said that the system of "graduation" in these groups is not good. In my opinion, that is not true. _____

Listening Dictation

CD を聞いて次の空欄を埋めましょう。

1. It is said that these groups provide a 1)(　　　　) role model for girls. In my opinion, that is not true. A 2)(　　　　) role model is a female singer-songwriter.

2. The members of these groups always make an 1)(　　　　) to meet and 2)(　　　　) the fans.

3. These groups are 1)(　　　　) for teenagers but I think it is a bit 2)(　　　　) for adults to like them.

UNIT 8

Speaking

次の会話モデルを使用して、クラスメートや先生にあなたの意見を伝えてください。また、先ほど学習した表現も積極的に使いましょう。

A Do you think that female pop groups such as _____ are a negative trend?

B Yes, I do.　OR　No, I don't.

A Why do you say that?

B [reason] _____

A It is said that _____

What do you think?

B In my opinion, that is not true. [*refutation] _____

A OK. I see.

B How about you? Do you think they are a negative trend?

A Yes, I do.　OR　No, I don't. [reason] _____

*refutation：反論

　　大人数からなるアイドルグループは昔から存在しているので、昨今のさまざまなグループの登場にさほど驚く人はいないかもしれません。ですが、世界に目を向けると、それは日本特有の現象と言えるでしょう。たとえば、日本以外で何十人もメンバーがいるアイドルグループを、あなたはいくつ思い浮かべることができるでしょうか。もしかしたらこの現象の裏には、日本人特有の気質が深く関わっているのかもしれません。

　ちなみに、あるインターネットのサイトで、「ちょうどいいと思うアイドルグループの人数」を聞いたところ、1位は断トツで「5人」(64%)、2位が「4人」(13%)、3位が「3人」(10%)という回答でした。

UNIT 9 Social Networking Services

今や世界中で大流行の SNS ですが、SNS には良い面だけでなく、悪い面があるのも事実のようです。あなたはどちらの面をより強く感じますか。

Vocabulary in Context

次の下線部に入る語を以下の語群から選んでください。

1. My friend has developed a(n) _____ online game for SNS users.
2. I like SNS because I can _____ lively discussions online with my friends.
3. Parents should _____ the risks before letting their children use SNS.
4. I don't like SNS because people add _____ comments to my pictures.
5. One _____ of social networks that people worry about is privacy.
6. Illegally downloading music from the internet is a kind of _____ .

   | aspect   conduct   original   consider   theft   stupid |

SNSは有益なメディアである

For

❶ Social networking services (SNS) such as Facebook, Twitter and LINE sometimes receive criticism about their negative effect on people's behavior. However, the truth is that they have many positive aspects.

❷ Firstly, these services are based on sharing. You take a picture, you share it. You do something cool, you tell everybody about it. Through using SNS, people learn the joy of sharing.

❸ In addition, SNS have the wonderful effect of boosting our egos. If, for example, you post a nice photo, many people will click on the "Like" button. Before you know it, you may have 30 or 40 "Likes." This is similar to receiving a big pat on the back.

❹ Finally, these services encourage people to express themselves in new and interesting ways. LINE for example offers hundreds of "stickers" that can be included in messages. Some people even conduct whole conversations using only stickers. Is that not an original form of communication?

Against

❺ Social networking services have experienced a boom in recent years. Although these services are very popular, they are encouraging young people to behave in negative ways.

❻ First of all, these services encourage addictive behavior. Many young people do not realize it but, in fact, they are addicted to SNS. They check messages several times an hour, instantly uploading photos of whatever they do and constantly scanning the services to find out what their friends are doing.

❼ Secondly, these services encourage egotistic behavior. For example, some people upload pictures of food they are about to eat in a restaurant. Is it not merely a subtle form of boasting?

❽ And thirdly, we must also consider the dangerous behaviors that SNS encourage. These include stalking and identity theft. Furthermore, some young people have used these services to share photos of themselves doing stupid or even illegal things at work.

Note

social networking service ソーシャルネットワーキングサービス（人と人との交流を支援するインターネット上のサービス）　**cool** すごい、かっこいい（米口語）　**boost one's ego** 〜の自尊心を高める　**post ~** 〜を投稿する　**"Like"**「いいね！」　**a big pat on the back** 大きな賞賛（patは「軽くたたくこと」の意味）　**"stickers"**「スタンプ」　**addictive** 中毒性の　**be addicted to ~** 〜の中毒になる、〜にやみつきになる　**upload ~** 〜をアップロードする（サーバーに転送すること）　**scan ~** 〜にざっと目を通す　**egotistic** 利己的な　**be about to do**（まさに）〜しようとしている　**stalking** ストーキング、ストーカー行為　**identity theft** 個人情報泥棒

Comprehension

次の文は本文の内容を要約したものです。該当する段落の番号を空欄に書き入れて、for または against のどちらかを○で囲んでください。

			for / against
1	We can express ourselves in original ways on SNS.		for / against
2	Some people become addicted to SNS.		for / against
3	Gaining "Likes" on SNS makes us feel good.		for / against
4	Some people seem to use SNS to boast about what they are doing.		for / against
5	SNS are a wonderful way to share things.		for / against
6	Some people use SNS in bad ways.		for / against

Grammar Point

分詞構文 の付帯状況

分詞構文の中で付帯状況が最も多く用いられる。この他に、時（〜すると）・理由（〜なので）・条件（〜ならば）・譲歩（〜だけれども）の意味を表す場合もある。

1. 動作の連続：「〜して、そして」

   *They check messages several times an hour, instantly **uploading** photos of whatever they do and constantly **scanning** the services to find out what their friends are doing.*

2. 動作の同時：「〜しながら」

   *Some people even conduct whole conversations **using** only stickers.*

UNIT 9

Writing

次の例文を参考にしながら、あなた自身の具体的な例を意見に盛り込む方法を学びましょう。

> One good point about SNS is sharing. **As for me**, I often share photos on SNS and also enjoy looking at my friends' photos.

このほかにも次のような言い方ができます。

> In my case, I ....

それでは、下欄の for か against を○で囲み、具体例を交えながらその理由を英語で書いてみましょう。

I am for / against   this proposal.

[reason] _____

In my case, _____

Listening Dictation

CD 28

CD を聞いて次の空欄を埋めましょう。

1. SNS can ¹⁾(　　　　) ²⁾(　　　　　) in positive ways. As for me I use them for learning and practicing English.

2. Some young people tend to ¹⁾(　　　　) communicating by SNS ²⁾(　　　　) talking face-to-face.

3. LINE is ¹⁾(　　　　) useful because it can be used ²⁾(　　　　) ³⁾(　　　　) email.

Speaking

次の会話モデルを使用して、クラスメートや先生にあなたの意見を伝えてください。また、先ほど学習した表現も積極的に使いましょう。

A Do you think SNS are a positive trend?

B Well… yes, I do   OR   no, I don't

A OK. Why do you say that?

B [reason] _____

A Anything else?

B [reason] _____

A I see. Thanks for explaining your opinions.

B How about you? What do you think?

A Well, I think they are a positive/negative trend.

B Could you explain why?

A Sure. [reason] _____

「SNS中毒」や「SNS 疲れ」という言葉が象徴するように、便利なはずのSNSが日本でも社会問題を引き起こしつつあります。また最近では、自分の子供の写真をSNSに大量にアップすることが、将来の親子トラブルの原因になるのではないかと危惧する声も上がっています。

そうした中、ある国際的な調査で世界の主要49カ国のネットユーザーにSNSの利用頻度を聞いたところ、意外なことに日本は最下位だったことが明らかになりました。ちなみに、「SNSを利用していない」と答えた人たちが語ったその主な理由は、「興味がないから」と「個人情報を知られたくないから」というものでした。

UNIT 10 Using Smartphones while Walking

歩きながらスマートフォンを操作する、いわゆる「歩きスマホ」が大きな問題になりつつあります。やめさせるには、いったいどうすればよいのでしょうか。

Vocabulary in Context

次の空欄に入る語を以下から選んでください。

1. There are smartphone *apps that can even _____ some diseases.
2. Using a smartphone or tablet too much can _____ a stiff neck.
3. The _____ should tackle smartphone theft. It is a big problem.
4. My smartphone is bright pink so it is very _____!
5. I have insurance in case I lose my smartphone or a(n) _____ steals it.
6. It is _____ to put your smartphone into manner mode on the train.

*app：アプリ（application software [program] の略）

| cause | authorities | visible | advisable | criminal | detect |

テーマ 歩きスマホは違法にすべきである

For

❶ People using smartphones while walking around town have become a common sight these days. For several reasons, we should consider making this behavior illegal.

❷ Firstly, of course, this behavior is very dangerous. People using smartphones while walking are a danger, not only to themselves but also to others. Some people have caused terrible car accidents by crossing the road when using a smartphone.

❸ Secondly, even if the authorities warn against this behavior, their advice is ignored. Unfortunately, many people pay no attention to mere warnings. The only way to change this life-threatening behavior is to make it illegal.

❹ Finally, an important aspect of the behavior is that it is very visible. These days many children have cellphones. They may see and then copy this behavior. We have to make it illegal to ensure that young children do not start to behave in the same way.

Against

❺ Walking and using a smartphone at the same time is not advisable but it is not an activity that should be made illegal.

❻ Firstly, many activities cause people to pay less attention to their surroundings. Some people daydream as they walk along. Others listen to music through headphones. Lovers gaze into each other's eyes as they walk hand in hand. Should these activities also be made illegal?

❼ Secondly, there are times when it may be unavoidable to use a smartphone while walking. For example, a busy working mother on the way to work might have to send a message to her child.

❽ And finally, making every little thing illegal is not a good approach. It turns many ordinary people into criminals. A better approach might be to have sensors in smartphones that detect walking. Then functions could automatically be limited when walking is detected.

UNIT 10

> **Note**
> **common sight** ありふれた光景　**life-threatening** 命にかかわる　**cellphone** 携帯電話（cellular phoneの略語）　**daydream** 空想にふける　**gaze in to each other's eyes** お互いの目をじっと見つめ合う　**hand in hand** 手をつないで　**on the way to work** 職場へ行く途中で（workは名詞で「職場・会社」の意味）　**every little thing** ほんのちょっとしたこと　**sensor** センサー

Comprehension

次の文は本文の内容を要約したものです。該当する段落の番号を空欄に書き入れて、for または against のどちらかを○で囲んでください。

1	It is dangerous to use a smartphone when walking.		for	against
2	Using a smartphone is not the only dangerous activity people do when walking.		for	against
3	Some people are so busy that they have to use a smartphone when walking.		for	against
4	Children might copy such behavior.		for	against
5	There are other approaches for dealing with this problem.		for	against
6	People respect only the law, not warnings.		for	against

Grammar Point

when の用法

1. **関係副詞**

   *Secondly, there are times **when** it may be unavoidable to use a smartphone while walking.*

   ▌whenはtimesを先行詞とする制限用法（限定用法）として用いられている。

2. **接続詞：「〜する時に」**

   (1) *Some people have caused terrible car accidents by crossing the road **when** using a smartphone.*

   (2) *Then functions could automatically be limited **when** walking is detected.*

Writing

次の例文を参考にして、**illegal** と **legal** の使い方を学習しましょう。

1. Using a smartphone while walking should be made **illegal**.
2. Making every little thing **illegal** is not a good approach.

ディベートやディスカッションでは、illegal という語と、その反対の legal という語がよく使用されます。次の例も参考にしてください。

3. Smoking should be made **illegal** because it is so dangerous.
4. Some types of gambling are **legal** in Japan.
5. Owning a gun is **legal** in America.

それでは、次の空欄に英語を書き入れて **6.** と **7.** の文を完成させましょう。

6. _____ is illegal in Japan.
7. _____ is legal in Japan.

最後に、下欄の agree / disagree と、should / should not をそれぞれ○で囲み、その理由を英語で書いてください。

> I agree / disagree with this proposal.
>
> Walking while using a smartphone should / should not be made illegal
>
> because ....
>
> ....

Listening Dictation

CD を聞いて次の空欄を埋めましょう。

1. It is illegal to use a smartphone while ¹⁾(　　　　　), so it should be the ²⁾(　　　　　) for walking.

2. I think this ¹⁾(　　　　　) on the location. In a pedestrian area it should be ²⁾(　　　　　).

3. ¹⁾(　　　　　) who was walking and texting at the same time bumped into me ²⁾(　　　　　).

UNIT 10

Speaking

次の会話モデルを使用して、クラスメートや先生にあなたの意見を伝えてみましょう。また、先ほど学習した表現も積極的に使いましょう。

A Do you think that walking and using a smartphone at the same time should be made illegal?

B Now that's a difficult question! Let me see. Well, I guess, yes, I do.   OR   no, I don't.

A OK. Could you explain why you think that way?

B Sure. [reason] _____

A I see. Anything else?

B [reason] _____

A Right.

B How about you? What do you think?

A Well, I (also) think it should (not) be made illegal.

B Why's that?

A [reason] _____

　　世界的に社会問題となっている「歩きスマホ」ですが、各国ではどのような対策が取られているのでしょうか。日本では、歩きスマホを検知すると警告画面が表示されて、スマートフォンが操作できなくなるアプリを、大手の通信事業者が無料配布しています。

　　またアメリカでは、2012年にニュージャージー州のフォートリーで、歩きスマホを禁止する条例がすでに成立していて、違反者には85ドル（約1万円）の罰金が科せられています。

　　最後にお隣の中国では、歩道の半分に線を引いた「歩きスマホ専用レーン」なるものが重慶市の中心部にあるようですが、大きな成果はあがっていないようです。

UNIT 11 iPhone vs. Android

今では、若い人のほとんどがスマートフォンを使用していますが、
あなたは iPhone 派ですか、それとも Android 派ですか。
また、その理由は何ですか。

Vocabulary in Context

次の空欄に入る語を以下から選んでください。

1. The picture quality of my phone's camera is _____ to a compact camera.

2. I will _____ get a new smartphone this year.

3. My favorite _____ is my smartphone. It's so useful for many things.

4. The best _____ of my smartphone is the big clear screen.

5. Apple products are not _____ . In fact, they are very easy to use.

6. A smartphone is not _____ expensive. Some models are very cheap.

> probably   complicated   device   necessarily   comparable   feature

iPhone は最高のスマートフォンである

[1] Most people reading this text probably have a smartphone. Without doubt, a large number of these will be iPhones. This is the best smartphone for the following reasons.

[2] Generally speaking, a smartphone is a very complicated device. In the past, smartphones were only for very advanced users. The iPhone, however, makes everything easy because it is so simple and intuitive. To put it simply, the iPhone is the easiest smartphone to use.

[3] In addition, the iPhone ecosystem works very well. Thousands of applications are available to download from the App Store. The phone synchronizes with music on your computer. Photos and videos can easily be shared. All in all, it is a very smooth experience.

[4] Finally, the iPhone is the coolest-looking smartphone. Apple is famous for designing appealing devices, thanks to the design philosophy of the late Steve Jobs. When you own a cool iPhone, you are also sharing his vision.

[5] Without doubt, the iPhone is a very good smartphone. It is not necessarily the best smartphone, however. Please consider the following points.

[6] Firstly, the iPhone is too expensive. It is more expensive than many comparable Android phones. Young people with a limited budget are advised to shop around and choose a more reasonably-priced Android phone.

[7] Secondly, iPhones all look the same. Imagine if everybody wore almost exactly the same clothes. It would be boring! If you choose an Android phone, there is a wide variety of models, so it is easier to find a color or design that you like.

[8] Finally, Android phones have some useful features not found in the iPhone range. One example is water resistance. Some Android phones are waterproof, which means that they can be used on rainy days and at the beach with no worries. Even if you drop them in water, they will be fine.

UNIT 11

> **Note**
> **intuitive** 直感的に理解できる　**to put it simply** 簡単に言えば　**ecosystem** エコシステム（本来は「生態系」の意味だが、ここでは端末・ソフトウェア・サービスなどから成る収益構造全体を指す）　**App Store** アップストア（アップル社が運営するアプリケーションソフトの販売サイト）　**synchronize with ~** ～を同期する　**all in all** 全体として　**appealing** 魅力的な　**design philosophy** デザイン哲学　**the late Steve Jobs** 故スティーブ・ジョブズ（1955-2011; アップル社の共同創立者の一人）　**shop around** いくつかの店を見てまわる　**range** 品ぞろえ　**water resistance** 防水性　**waterproof** 防水の（= water-resistant）

Comprehension

次の文は本文の内容を要約したものです。該当する段落の番号を空欄に書き入れて、for または against のどちらかを○で囲んでください。

①	The iPhone looks very stylish.		for	against
②	The iPhone is very simple to use.		for	against
③	Android phones have some unique features.		for	against
④	Many Android phones are relatively cheaper.		for	against
⑤	The iPhone ecosystem is excellent.		for	against
⑥	The iPhone range lacks variety.		for	against

Grammar Point

however の位置

> however は文頭・文中・文末のいずれにも用いられるので、和訳する時には、注意が必要となる。

（文頭）**However**, a smartphone is a very complicated device.
（文中）*The iPhone, **however**, makes everything easy because it is so simple and intuitive.*
（文末）*It is not necessarily the best smartphone, **however**.*

UNIT 11

Writing

次の例文を参考にして、比較級と最上級の表現を学習しましょう。

1. The iPhone is **the easiest** smartphone to use.
2. The iPhone is **the coolest**-looking smartphone.
3. The iPhone is **more expensive than** most Android phones.
4. Android phones are **better than** the iPhone because there are more designs.

比較級と最上級を作る際には、規則変化と不規則変化があることを改めて確認しておきましょう。

規則変化 ： cute → cuter → cutest
　　　　　　simple → simpler → simplest
　　　　　　expensive → more expensive → most expensive

不規則変化 ： good → better → best
　　　　　　　bad → worse → worst

下欄の for か against を○で囲み、比較級か最上級を使って空欄を英語で埋めましょう。

I am for / against this proposal.
_____
_____

Listening Dictation

CD を聞いて次の空欄を埋めましょう。

1. The iPhone is the best smartphone for taking photos. The 1)(　　　　) on my iPhone is easy to use and takes very 2)(　　　　) pictures.

2. My Android phone seems to be very 1)(　　　　) ; even when I dropped it, it didn't 2)(　　　　).

3. I 1)(　　　　) to use a "Galapagos" phone because it is cheaper and 2)(　　　　).

Speaking

次の会話モデルを使用して、クラスメートや先生にあなたの意見を伝えてみましょう。また、先ほど学習した表現も積極的に使いましょう。

A Do you think that (the iPhone/Android phones) is/are the best smartphone?

B Well,… yes, I do.   OR   no, I don't.

A Really? Why's that?

B [reason] _____

A But don't you think that (the iPhone/Android phones) is/are cooler than (the iPhone/Android phones)?

B No, not really. [reason] _____

A OK, I see.

B How about you? What do you think?

A I think that the iPhone is best (too).   OR   I think that Android phones are best (too). [reason] _____

　　世界中のすべての国を調べたわけではないようですが、ある調査によると、AndroidのシェアをiPhoneが上回った国は日本だけだったそうです。ちなみに理由は不明ですが、例えばスペインは、約9割の人がAndroidを使用しています。

　　そしてこの逆転現象の裏には、iPhoneの価格が関係しているようです。世界的に見ると、iPhoneは気軽に手を出すことのできない高級品であるの対して、Androidは安価で幅広いユーザー向け端末と位置づけられています。しかし日本では、海外ほど両者の間に価格差はありません。どうやらこうした事実が、先ほどの調査結果に少なからず影響を及ぼしているようです。

UNIT 12 Video Gaming

最近、家庭用ゲーム機や携帯型ゲーム機さらにはスマホを使ってゲームをしている人が増えているようですが、あなたもその一人ですか。ゲームをしないという人は、暇な時に何をしていますか。

Vocabulary in Context

次の空欄に入る語を以下から選んでください。

1. Gaming has many good points. Don't _____ it so easily!
2. My parents _____ the time I play games to just one hour per day.
3. Some online games have a(n) _____ of cooperation.
4. I had a long gaming _____ last night. I went to bed at 2 am.
5. You look _____. Were you gaming again last night?
6. Watching movies is too _____. Games are more interactive.

> limit   session   tired   dismiss   passive   element

ゲームで遊ぶのは時間の無駄である

1 These days, it is gaming that many young people spend most of their time on. However, although it may be hard for gamers to accept, they are in fact wasting their time. Let's think about why.

2 In the first place, gaming does not stretch our minds or give us something to think deeply about. It is a kind of mental junk food. When you do a lot of gaming, instead of developing your mind, you allow your mind to stagnate.

3 Secondly, gaming is not an activity that is over in a few minutes. Many young people cannot limit the time they play. One session can easily last for two or three hours or more. That is a big waste of time!

4 And finally, gaming does not provide any tangible result. Other pastimes such as painting or cooking create nice final products. Unfortunately, from gaming, there is nothing except tired eyes and a stiff neck.

5 When gaming is discussed, many non-gamers dismiss it as a waste of time. This is unfair. There are positive aspects to gaming and these must also be considered.

6 Firstly, gaming teaches us many useful skills—things such as the ability to react quickly and the ability to think ahead. Developing such skills can be useful in real life, for driving or for operating machines at work or for other practical things.

7 Secondly, many games are now online games. People play cooperatively with friends and also make new friends, even in other countries. We can chat while gaming, and that is great communication. Nobody can say that making friends and communicating with them is a waste of time.

8 Finally, many young people these days are said to be too passive and uncompetitive. Gaming has an element of competition which can invigorate young people and make them become more competitive in their daily lives.

UNIT 12

Note

stretch one's mind ～の知性を伸ばす　**junk food** ジャンクフード（カロリーが高いだけで栄養価は低いスナック）　**stagnate** 成長が止まる　**tangible** 具体的な、触れることのできる　**stiff neck** 肩こり　**think ahead** 先のことを考える　**cooperatively** 協力して　**chat** チャットする（ネットワーク上でおしゃべりする）　**uncompetitive** 競争しない　**invigorate ~** ～を刺激する

Comprehension

次の文は本文の内容を要約したものです。該当する段落の番号を空欄に書き入れて、for または against のどちらかを○で囲んでください。

			for/against
1	Many young people spend too much time playing video games.		for / against
2	Video gaming does not create something.		for / against
3	Various skills can be learned from gaming.		for / against
4	Video games can make passive youngsters more competitive.		for / against
5	Gaming does not exercise our brains.		for / against
6	We can make friends and communicate with people through games.		for / against

Grammar Point

強調構文 : It is ~ that … 「…なのは~である」

[It is ~ that …] の~の部分に文中の一部を入れると、その部分が強調される。

*These days, **it is** gaming **that** many young people spend most of their time on.*

強調構文と形式主語構文の見分け方
It is と that 以外の語句で語順を変えるなどして、文として成立すれば強調構文となる。

例 1. **It is** this hospital **that** my father visits every Friday. （強調構文）
　　 2. **It is** true **that** she bought a new house. （形式主語構文）

Writing

次の例文を参考にして、現在時制の正しい用法を学習しましょう。

1. Gaming **does not stretch** our minds.
2. Painting and cooking **create** nice final products.
3. Gaming **teaches** us many useful skills.

日本語と同様に、「真理・社会通念」といった普遍的な事柄は、現在形で表します。趣味などについて話し合う時によく使われるので、もう少し例を挙げておきます。

4. Reading **improves** our vocabulary.
5. Watching foreign movies **broadens** our horizons.
6. Gambling **wastes** money.

それでは下欄の agree か disagree を○で囲み、現在時制を使って空欄を英語で埋めてください。なお、現在時制を使って答えるのが難しい場合は、これまでの章で学んだものを使用しましょう。

I agree / disagree with this proposal.

___

___

Listening Dictation

 37

CD を聞いて次の空欄を埋めましょう。

1. Gaming creates many problems. For example, gamers often do not get 1)(　　　) sleep and seem to be 2)(　　　) all the time.

2. The gaming industry 1)(　　　) many 2)(　　　) for people such as programmers and artists.

3. I'm not a big gamer but I do like playing 1)(　　　) games on my smartphone to kill 2)(　　　).

UNIT 12

Speaking

次の会話モデルを使用して、クラスメートや先生にあなたの意見を伝えてみましょう。また、先ほど学習した表現も積極的に使いましょう。

A Do you play video games?

B Yes, a lot/a little.　OR　No, not much/not at all.

A Do you think gaming is a waste of time?

B Good question! Well, I guess... yes, I do.　OR　no, I don't.

A OK. Why do you say that?

B [reason] _____

A Anything else?

B [reason] _____

A Thanks. I understand.

B How about you? What do you think?

A I think gaming is / is not a waste of time (too). [reason] _____
_____

Column

　一般にゲームは否定的に捉えられる傾向にありますが、その一方で、英会話の習得にオンラインゲームがとても役に立ったという声もあります。

　本文中にも少し書かれていましたが、もし海外の人たちと一緒にオンラインゲームをプレイすれば、会話のほとんどは英語で行われます。もしゲーム中に相手の指示がよく理解できなかったり、自分から指示がうまく伝えられなければ、ゲームの楽しさは半減してしまいます。そんな時、オンラインゲームをもっと楽しみたいという気持ちが、その後の英会話学習のモチベーションとなる人も少なくないようです。

UNIT 13 Celebrating Foreign Festivals

クリスマスやバレンタインデーといった外国の風習は、今や日本に完全に定着しました。あなたはこうした状況を歓迎しますか。それとも何か違和感を覚えますか。

Vocabulary in Context

次の下線部に入る語を以下の語群から選んでください。

1. Christmas is _____ ! We can have a party and exchange presents.
2. Some people _____ the *commercialization of Christmas.
3. Is Easter a happy or a sad festival? I feel a little _____ about it.
4. It is _____ to give children too many expensive presents at Christmas.
5. Recently, there has been a(n) _____ in Japan for young women to buy chocolates for themselves on Valentine's Day.
6. We _____ Halloween on October 31st.

*commercialization：商業化

| celebrate | fun | trend | wrong | confused | criticize |

外国のお祭りを祝うのは良いことである

❶ Globalization has brought many new trends to Japan. One result of this is that many Japanese people now celebrate foreign festivals such as Christmas, Halloween and Valentine's Day. This is a good thing for the following reasons.

❷ Firstly, these festivals are fun. They bring joy and excitement to many people. Furthermore, because they are not traditional Japanese events, they can be enjoyed more freely.

❸ Another point is that foreign festivals stimulate the Japanese economy. On these occasions, people like to buy things, go out to restaurants or have a party. All of these activities can help local businesses.

❹ Finally, international cultural exchange is a positive trend. We are happy to hear that people around the world are enjoying Japanese culture such as manga and anime. In a similar way, it is also good for us to enjoy foreign culture, traditions and festivals.

❺ Japan is primarily a Shinto-Buddhist country. As such, it is wrong for Japanese people to eagerly celebrate Christmas, Halloween, Valentine's Day and other similar festivals.

❻ The first point is that, by celebrating such festivals, we may lose touch with our roots. For example, if families celebrate Halloween with more energy than *Setsubun*, Japanese children may become confused about their identity.

❼ Secondly, many people in Japan do not understand the meaning behind these festivals. Given this fact, foreign people may criticize us for frivolously celebrating Christian festivals that have little or no connection to Japan.

❽ Finally, we should be proud of our own culture and traditions. They have been handed down to us by our ancestors and connect us to Japan's long history. Let's celebrate our culture by celebrating our own festivals more strongly. And let's invite our foreign friends to come and enjoy our festivals too!

> **Note**
> **globalization** 国際化、グローバル化　**stimulate ~** ~を刺激する　**local businesses** 地元企業　**international cultural exchange** 国際文化交流　**in a similar way** 同様に　**Shinto-Buddhist country** 神道と仏教の国（神道とは、日本固有の民族信仰として伝承されてきた多神教の宗教のこと）　**as such** そういうわけで、そのため　**lose touch with ~** ~と接触がなくなる、疎遠になる　**roots** ルーツ（人の民族的・文化的な起源）　**frivolously** 面白半分に　**be handed down to ~** ~に伝えられる

Comprehension

次の文は本文の内容を要約したものです。該当する段落の番号を空欄に書き入れて、for または against のどちらかを◯で囲んでください。

			for / against
1	Celebrating foreign festivals is a positive kind of cultural exchange.		for / against
2	We should be proud of our own festivals.		for / against
3	Many people do not understand the meaning of these festivals.		for / against
4	These festivals can help the economy.		for / against
5	Foreign festivals are enjoyed by many people.		for / against
6	We might lose our own traditions.		for / against

Grammar Point

given の使い方

***Given** this fact, foreign people may criticize us for frivolously celebrating Christian festivals that have little or no connection to Japan.*

> 条件を表す分詞構文が慣用化したもの。ここでは前置詞的に用いられ「~を考えれば、~を考慮に入れると」という意味になる。また次の例のように、that節を伴うこともある。

例 Given that he is inexperienced, he has done a good job.

UNIT 13

Writing

次の例文を参考にして、"**By + 動名詞**"の使い方を学習しましょう。

1. **By celebrating** foreign festivals, we can have fun.
2. **By celebrating** foreign festivals, children may become confused.
3. **By enjoying** foreign festivals, we can learn about other cultures.

同じような表現方法として、次のようなものもあります。

4. **Thanks to** foreign festivals, we..

「〜のおかげで」という意味です。通常、肯定的に物事を述べる際に使われます。

それでは、for か against を○で囲んで、空白部分を英語で埋めてみましょう。

I am for / against this proposal.

By celebrating foreign festivals, we _____

_____

_____

Listening Dictation

CD 40

CD を聞いて次の空欄を埋めましょう。

1. By celebrating such festivals, people might ¹⁾(   ) too ²⁾(   ) money.

2. ¹⁾(   ) festivals help us to understand foreign ²⁾(   ).

3. Foreign festivals ¹⁾(   ) people ²⁾(   ) together.

UNIT 13

Speaking

次の会話モデルを使用して、クラスメートや先生にあなたの意見を伝えてみましょう。また、先ほど学習した表現も積極的に使いましょう。

A Do you think it's good to celebrate foreign festivals in Japan?

B Yes, I think so.   OR   No, I don't think so.

A Why do you say that?

B [reason] _____

A OK, I see. Any other reasons?

B Also, _____
_____

A That's interesting.

B How about you? What do you think?

A As for me, I think it's good.   OR   As for me, I don't think it's so good.

B Why do you say that?

A [reason] _____

　日本で最初のクリスマスは、なんと戦国時代までさかのぼります。キリスト教が伝来した3年後の1552年のクリスマスの日に、周防国（現在の山口県）で宣教師が信徒を招いてミサを開いたという記録が残っています。日本のクリスマスには想像以上に長い歴史がありますが、欧米のクリスマスとはどのように異なっているのでしょうか。

　昔から欧米では、クリスマスは家族が一緒に過ごす日と決まっています。普段は恋人や友人との約束を優先させる子供たちも、この日はずっと家にいて、家族とゆっくり食事を楽しみながらイエス・キリストの誕生を祝います。

　またクリスマスディナーはと言うと、英国の場合、詰め物をした七面鳥の丸焼き、ローストポテト、蒸した野菜、そしてデザートにクリスマス・プディング（ドライフルーツやナッツなどを入れて蒸した黒い色のケーキ）がよく食べられます。イチゴののった白いケーキとローストチキンが食卓に並ぶ日本とは、似ているようでまったく違うものとなっています。

UNIT 14 Eating on the Train

あるデータによると、電車内でものを食べる人が最近増えているようです。マナーの問題として、どこまでなら許されるとあなたは思いますか。

Vocabulary in Context

次の空欄に入る語を以下から選んでください。また必要に応じて語の形を変化させましょう。

1. My current job _____ my personality.
2. There are often rude people on the train, but I just _____ them.
3. Playing games on my smartphone is a kind of _____ for me after a busy day.
4. _____ trains are much more comfortable than older ones.
5. I have a lot of _____ at work, so I listen to music on the train to relax.
6. Sometimes there are _____ smells on the train.

> pressure   modern   suit   ignore   unpleasant   escape

テーマ 電車内でものを食べても構わない

 For

1 Twenty or thirty years ago, it was unthinkable to eat food on a local train. Nowadays, however, we quite often see people doing so. Is it acceptable? I think that, yes, it is. I have three reasons.

2 Firstly, people are very busy these days. Society puts a lot of pressure on us and we must always rush to be on time or to meet deadlines. For some people, commuting time is the only time they have for eating.

3 Secondly, many modern foods are neatly wrapped and the perfect size for eating quietly on the train. Bite-sized sandwiches are a good example. Of course, it also depends on the smell, but many snacks hardly smell at all.

4 Finally, social manners are not written in stone. Manners should be adapted to suit modern lifestyles. Therefore, instead of saying that eating on trains should be banned, we should consider what good manners for eating on trains are.

 Against

5 Good manners have always been important. The famous quote, "manners maketh man," was written almost 500 years ago! However, these days, manners are slipping and one example is eating on the train. This behavior is wrong for the following reasons.

6 If you eat on the train, other people cannot help but look. The action itself is impossible to ignore. It is not pleasant for those who are forced to watch and it is not pleasant to be watched. The whole situation is wrong.

7 Also, there are problems with the noise and smell. The sound of someone chomping is unpleasant. And if the food has a strong smell, that is unpleasant, too. There is no escape for those who are not eating.

8 The final point is respect. Manners show that we respect each other. However, eating on the train seems to indicate that we do not care about other people. It is selfish and inconsiderate behavior.

UNIT 14

> **Note**
>
> **local train**（各駅停車の）普通列車　**meet deadlines** 締切に間に合わせる（meetには「（要求・期待などを）満たす」という意味がある）　**commuting time** 通勤（通学）時間　**bite-sized** 一口サイズの　**be not written in stone**（石に刻まれたように）変えられないものではない　"**manners maketh man**"「礼儀は人を作る（人は礼儀作法で判断できる）」（makethはmakeの古い表現）　**slip** 低下する　**cannot help but do** ～せずにはいられない（cannot help doing と言い換えることもできる。また、helpは「避ける」という意味で使用されている）　**chomp** ものをかむ　**inconsiderate** 配慮のない、礼儀をわきまえない

Comprehension

次の文は本文の内容を要約したものです。該当する段落の番号を空欄に書き入れて、for または against のどちらかを○で囲んでください。

1	Eating food is noisy and creates a strong smell on the train.		for	against
2	Eating food on the train seems to show that we do not think about other people.		for	against
3	We have to change manners to fit in with our lifestyles.		for	against
4	These days, snacks are small and neat and do not smell so much.		for	against
5	People are so busy that they have to eat on the train.		for	against
6	Eating on the train is a very conspicuous activity.		for	against

Grammar Point

一般的な人々を表す　those (who)

1. *It is not pleasant for **those who** are forced to watch...*
2. *There is no escape for **those who** are not eating.*

> those は「それらのもの（人）」という意味だが、関係代名詞whoを伴うと「…である人々」を表す。また、those present（出席者）やthose concerned（関係者）のように、関係詞節以外の形容詞（句）が使用されることもある。

UNIT 14

Writing

次の2つの例文を参考にして、"**depend on**" の使い方を学習しましょう。

> **depend on ~** で「~による、~次第である」という意味になります。これを使うことで、自分の意見にさらに幅を持たせたり、より正確に自分の立場を相手に伝えることができます。

1. Some people say it is acceptable to eat on trains. I agree but I think it **depends on** the time of day. It is OK when there are not many people, but during the rush hour it is not good.

2. Some people say it is acceptable to eat on trains. I disagree but also I suppose it **depends on** the time of day. When the train is empty it might be OK.

それでは、agree か disagree を◯で囲んで空白部分を英語で埋めてみましょう。

> Some people say that it is acceptable to eat on the train. I agree / disagree with this proposal, but I think it depends on _____
>
> _____

Listening Dictation

43

CDを聞いて次の空欄を埋めましょう。

1. Surely it depends on the type and size of the snack. I think eating small things such as 1)(   ) or 2)(   ) on the train is acceptable.

2. 1)(   ) you eat on the train 2)(   ) there is a risk of dropping the food on the floor.

3. To be 1)(   ), I 2)(   ) a snack on the train this morning.

UNIT 14

Speaking

次の会話モデルを使用して、クラスメートや先生にあなたの意見を伝えてみましょう。また、先ほど学習した表現も積極的に使いましょう。

A Do you think it is acceptable to eat on the train?

B Well,… yes, I do.   OR   no, I don't.

A Why do you think it is acceptable/unacceptable?

B [reason] _____

A I see. Any other reasons?

B Yes. [reason] _____

A OK.

B But, also, it depends on _____
_____

A Sure.

B How about you? What do you think?

A I think it's acceptable/unacceptable. [reason] _____

　電車内の飲食は日本ではマナーの問題ですが、海外にはそうした行為に厳しい罰則を設けている国があります。

　チューインガムの国内持ち込み禁止など、ルールに厳しい国としても有名なシンガポールでは、当然のことながら電車内での飲食は禁止されています。違反すると、500シンガポールドル（約44,000円）の罰金が科されます。

　また、意外かも知れませんが、屋台などでの「歩き食い文化」が盛んな台湾でも電車内での飲食は厳しく禁止されています。駅のホームや電車内で飲食すると、1,500元（約5,700円）以上7,500元（約29,000円）以下の罰金となります。なんとペットボトルの水やアメも罰金の対象となるようなので、旅行に行く際は注意しましょう。

UNIT 15 Ramen

ラーメンが苦手という人はめったにいないと思いますが、その栄養バランスに不安を感じる人は少なくないかもしれません。あなたにとって、ラーメンはどんな食べ物ですか。

Vocabulary in Context

次の空欄に入る語を以下から選んでください。また必要に応じて語の形を変化させましょう。

1. Ramen contains quite a large _____ of fat.
2. I tend to _____ health advice that I read in the newspapers.
3. I eat out a lot so I often _____ my monthly food budget.
4. _____ speaking, ramen is a reasonably-priced dish.
5. We _____ have ramen. Maybe once every two or three months.
6. My local ramen shop owner _____ that his ramen is the best in town!

| exceed | amount | generally | claim | disregard | occasionally |

ラーメンは体に良くないので食べないほうがよい

❶ Ramen may well be Japan's favorite food. However, despite its popularity, this dish is too unhealthy and therefore cannot be recommended.

❷ Firstly, calories. A bowl of ramen purchased in a ramen shop can contain more than 1,000 calories. That is a lot just for one meal and, with a side order of gyoza dumplings, the total can even exceed 1,500 calories.

❸ In addition, we must also consider salt. The recommended sodium intake for an adult is about 2,300mg per day. A single bowl of restaurant-served ramen can contain over 2,500mg of sodium—a very unhealthy amount, especially for people with high blood pressure.

❹ Finally, a bowl of ramen is generally not a balanced meal. It is high in fat and carbohydrates, but low in fiber, vitamins and minerals.

❺ For these reasons, ramen should be considered an unhealthy food and generally avoided.

❻ Some people say that ramen is unhealthy, but these claims can be disregarded for the following reasons.

❼ First of all, ramen is not a dish that is eaten every day. For most people, a trip to the ramen shop is a treat that they enjoy occasionally. As part of our monthly diet, eating two or three bowls of ramen is no problem at all.

❽ Secondly, although it may be true that ramen noodles and soup are high in calories, the toppings on the other hand are low in calories and healthy. Menma, for example, is made from bamboo shoots. And both nori seaweed and Japanese scallions are very healthy food items.

❾ The final point is that ramen is a wonderful comfort food. A delicious bowl of ramen at a good ramen shop has a very positive mental effect. It cheers us up and helps us forget our worries—and for a very reasonable price.

Note

dish 食べ物、料理　**a bowl of ~** １杯の～　**side order** 追加注文　**sodium** ナトリウム（食塩に含まれる成分のひとつ）　**intake** 摂取量　**restaurant-served** 店で出される　**high blood pressure** 高血圧　**fat** 脂肪　**carbohydrate** 炭水化物　**fiber** 食物繊維　**topping** 上にのせる具材、トッピング　**bamboo shoot** タケノコ　**Japanese scallion** 青ネギ　**comfort food** 元気の出る食べ物、なつかしい味（comfortには「慰めを与えてくれるもの」という意味がある）

Comprehension

次の文は本文の内容を要約したものです。該当する段落の番号を空欄に書き入れて、for または against のどちらかを○で囲んでください。

			for	against
1	Ramen toppings are healthy.		for	against
2	Ramen is high in calories.		for	against
3	It is hard to get a balanced meal from a bowl of ramen.		for	against
4	Ramen contains a lot of salt.		for	against
5	Most people do not eat ramen so often.		for	against
6	Eating ramen has positive mental benefits.		for	against

Grammar Point

may well ＋動詞の原形

以下の1.と2.の意味があるので、文脈で判断する必要がある。

1. 「たぶん（おそらく）〜だろう」（may よりも可能性が高い）

   Ramen **may well** be Japan's favorite food.

2. 「〜するのはもっともだ」（当然）

   You **may well** be surprised at the news.

UNIT 15

Writing

次の2つの例文を参考にして、"on the other hand" の使い方を学習しましょう。

> on the other hand は「他方では」を意味し、相手の意見に反対したり、自分の意見を弁護する際に役に立ちます。

1. Although ramen is high in calories, the toppings **on the other hand** are low in calories and healthy.

2. Ramen might be a good comfort food but, **on the other hand**, there are many healthier foods that can cheer us up.

下欄の for か against を○で囲み、どちらか一方を英語で埋めてください。

I am for / against this proposal.

FOR : Ramen might taste good but on the other hand _____

_____

AGAINST : Although ramen is high in calories, on the other hand _____

_____

Listening Dictation

CD を聞いて次の空欄を埋めましょう。

1. Ramen might be unhealthy but, on the other hand, a good point 1)(   ) ramen shops is 2)(   ) they are friendly places with a nice atmosphere.

2. Ramen can be quite expensive, 1)(   ) if you have 2)(   ) dishes such as gyoza dumplings.

3. I like meat so when I 1)(   ) ramen I always 2)(   ) the pork *chashu* type.

Speaking

次の会話モデルを使用して、クラスメートや先生にあなたの意見を伝えてみましょう。また、先ほど学習した表現も積極的に使いましょう。

A Do you think we should avoid eating ramen?

B Ramen? Well,… yes, I do.   OR   no, I don't.

A OK. Why do you say that?

B [reason] _____

A But don't you think it tastes good?

OR

But don't you think it is very high in calories?

B Maybe, but on the other hand _____
_____

A I see.

B How about you? What do you think?

A I (also) think we should avoid it because _____

OR

I think it is fine to eat ramen (too) because _____

　　　今や海外でも大人気のラーメンですが、長く食べ続けるためには注意すべきことがあるようです。まず、体に良いラーメンの食べ方としておすすめなのが、食べる順番です。「野菜→タンパク質（チャーシュー・卵）→炭水化物（めん）」の順に食べると、体への負担が軽減されると言われています。

　　　また、人によっては大変難しいことかもしれませんが、ラーメンの汁は半分以上残すことが基本です。もしスープがあまりに美味しすぎて、全部飲み干してしまった場合には、新鮮な野菜や果物に多く含まれるカリウムを摂取すると、余分なナトリウムが排出されるそうです。皆さんも是非試してみてください。

UNIT 16 Bread vs. Rice

忙しくて朝は食べないという人が増えていますが、あなたは朝食にはパンとごはん、どちらを食べることが多いですか。また、その理由は何ですか。

Vocabulary in Context

次の空欄に入る語を以下から選んでください。

1. A(n) _____ has shown that 40 percent of young people do not have breakfast.

2. People say that breakfast is the most important _____ of the day.

3. I _____ like having waffles with maple syrup for breakfast.

4. Japanese green tea is _____ refreshing and healthy.

5. There is only one slice of bread _____ . Do you want it?

6. Young people should have a(n) _____ and nourishing breakfast every day.

| survey | especially | remaining | meal | wonderfully | substantial |

テーマ 朝食はご飯よりもパンである

1 According to a recent survey of Japanese people who eat breakfast, almost 50 percent have bread and only about 36 percent have rice. Bread is certainly more popular and, in fact, is a better choice for the following reasons.

2 Firstly, bread is delicious. There are many types of bread and it can be prepared in many ways. A simple sandwich, for example, can have an almost infinite variety of fillings.

3 Secondly, bread is easier. It takes less time to prepare and even making toast is simple and quick. These days we are always rushing, especially in the morning. Bread is good for people who are very busy with work or studies.

4 Finally, it is easy to store any remaining bread—just seal the wrapper. It does not need to be covered in cellophane wrap and placed in the refrigerator. Furthermore, bread keeps well. One loaf can be used over several days.

5 Bread might be popular these days but that does not mean it is the best choice for breakfast. In some cases, the old ways are the best, and this applies to the first meal of the day.

6 To start with, rice is delicious. The combination of rice and miso soup, together with other traditional items, is a wonderfully simple but tasty way to start the morning.

7 Secondly, rice is better because it fills you up more. Have a delicious bowl of rice, and you will not feel hungry during the morning and therefore you will not be tempted to have any snacks. That is good for people who are watching their weight.

8 Finally, gram for gram, rice is cheaper than bread. Even if we include the costs of water and electricity for cooking, rice is still cheaper. Over the course of a year, this can add up to a substantial cost saving.

UNIT 16

> **Note**
> **filling** 具材　**seal ~** 〜に封をする　**wrapper** 袋、包み　**cellophane wrap** ラップ　**old ways** 昔からの習慣　**together with ~** 〜と共に　**fill ~ up** 〜を満腹にする　**be tempted to do** 〜したくなる（temptは「誘惑する」の意味）　**watch one's weight** 体重が増えないように気をつける（watchは「注意する」の意味）　**gram for gram** グラム単位では　**over the course of ~** 〜の間に　**add up to ~** 結局〜となる　**cost saving** コスト削減

Comprehension

次の文は本文の内容を要約したものです。該当する段落の番号を空欄に書き入れて、for または against のどちらかを○で囲んでください。

1	It is easy to prepare a bread-based breakfast.		for	against
2	Rice costs less than bread.		for	against
3	Bread tastes good.		for	against
4	Rice tastes good.		for	against
5	Rice stops us feeling hungry.		for	against
6	Bread can be kept easily in the kitchen and used for several days.		for	against

Grammar Point

命令文 **+ and**

Have *a delicious bowl of rice,* ***and*** *you will not feel hungry during the morning and therefore you will not be tempted to have any snacks.*

> 命令文の後で and が使用されると「そうすれば…」という意味になる。また、次の例文のように、or が使われると「さもないと…」という意味になる。

> 例 **Go** to bed now, **or** you won't be able to get up early tomorrow morning.

Writing

次の例文を参考にして、「Aは…にとって良い（悪い）ものだ」という言い方を学びましょう。

> A is good (bad) for people who are… .

1. Bread **is good for people who are** very busy with work or studies.
2. Rice **is good for people who are** watching their weight.

以下のように、関係代名詞の who を使わずにシンプルな文にすることもできます。

3. Bread **is good for** busy people.
4. Rice **is good for** losing weight.

それでは、下欄の agree か disagree を○で囲み、上の表現方法を使って空欄を英語で埋めてください。なお、上の形を使って答えるのが難しい場合は、これまでの章で学んだものを使用しましょう。

> I agree / disagree with this proposal.
> _____
> _____

Listening Dictation

CD を聞いて次の空欄を埋めましょう。

1. Some ¹⁾(　　　　) of bread such as wholegrain are good for people who need more ²⁾(　　　　) in their diet.

2. If we eat rice, we can also help to ¹⁾(　　　　) farmers in our ²⁾(　　　　).

3. ¹⁾(　　　　) for me, some days I have bread and other days I have rice. I like ²⁾(　　　　).

UNIT 16

Speaking

次の会話モデルを使用して、クラスメートや先生にあなたの意見を伝えてみましょう。また、先ほど学習した表現も積極的に使いましょう。

A Do you think that bread is a better option for breakfast than rice?

B Now, that's a tricky question. Well,… yes, I do.　　OR　　no, I don't.

A OK. Could you give me your reasons?

B Sure. [reason] _____

A Anything else?

B Also, [reason] _____

A Thanks. I understand.

B How about you? What do you think?

A I think bread is better (too).　　OR　　I think rice is better (too).

B Why's that?

A [reason] _____

B OK. By the way, what did you have for breakfast this morning?

A _____

本文にあった調査では、朝食が「パン派」の人は約50％で、「ごはん派」(36％)の人をわずかに上回る結果となりました。ですが一方、「本当はどちらを食べたいか」という別の調査では、「朝食にはごはんを食べたい」と答えた人が88％で圧倒的でした。どうやら、「朝はごはんを食べたいけれど、手間がかかるのでパンを食べている」というのが、多くの人々にとっての現実のようです。今ごはんに求められているのは、パンのような手軽さなのかもしれません。

UNIT 17 Blood Types

海外と比較して、日本では血液型の話がよく人々の話題に上がります。
あなたは血液型と性格には関係があると思いますか、
それとも単なる迷信だと思いますか。

Vocabulary in Context

次の空欄に入る語を以下から選んでください。

1. A(n) _____ of mine is blood type AB minus. That's rare!
2. Her _____ is typical for a type O person; confident but a little selfish.
3. He is so _____ . He often makes things by himself.
4. Blood type is a(n) _____ risk factor for some diseases.
5. I chose to study psychology because I like to _____ people.
6. Can my blood type _____ my future?

| personality analyze practical acquaintance significant affect |

UNIT 17

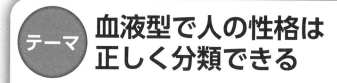

テーマ 血液型で人の性格は正しく分類できる

 50

For

1 Although it might be criticized as being pseudoscience, there is a lot of evidence indicating that blood types can be used to categorize personalities.

2 Firstly, consider personal experience. Many people notice that their friends' personalities match the standard blood type-personality categories. For example, type-A people are often observed to be fastidious, and type-B people are indeed "going their own way."

3 Secondly, there does seem to be some statistical evidence for the categories. For example, did you know that O-type people are said to be confident and strong-willed? Well, now consider the fact that 17 of Japan's prime ministers since World War Ⅱ have been blood type O.

4 Finally, analyzing blood types has proved to be useful for practical purposes. For example, couples have been successfully matched through blood types, and companies have used blood types to help screen candidates applying for vacant positions.

 51

Against

5 In the past, people in Japan and in other countries were very superstitious. Now, times have changed and we can disregard the old superstitions. That includes blood types.

6 Firstly, consider personal experience. Many people notice that, although a few of their friends may match blood type-personality categories, most do not. Furthermore, many acquaintances have a mix of personality traits from several different categories.

7 Secondly, large-scale scientific research involving thousands of people has not found a link between blood types and personality. If the existence of such a link is tested under strict scientific conditions, a significant relationship is not found.

8 Finally, in biological terms, blood type is decided by antigens or proteins found on the surface of red blood cells. How on earth could that affect personality? There is no biological mechanism for this.

Note

pseudoscience 偽科学（科学的根拠がないとされる理論や法則など; pseudo-は接頭辞で「偽りの、疑似の」の意味） **blood type-personality categories** 血液型性格分類 **fastidious** 気難しい **"go one's own way"** 「我が道を行く、自分の好きなようにやって行く」 **strong-willed** 意志の強い **prime minister** 総理大臣 **World War II** 第二次世界大戦（= the Second World War） **for practical purposes** 実用面で、実際に **screen ~** ~をふるいにかける **vacant position** 欠員 **superstitious** 迷信深い（名詞形はsuperstitionで「迷信」の意味） **large-scale** 大規模な **in biological terms** 生物学的に言えば **antigen** 抗原（生体内で抗体を形成させる物質） **red blood cell** 赤血球

Comprehension

次の文は本文の内容を要約したものです。該当する段落の番号を空欄に書き入れて、for または against のどちらかを○で囲んでください。

1	Most friends do not match blood type-personality categories.		for	against
2	Analyzing blood types has many uses.		for	against
3	Blood types have no biological connection to personality.		for	against
4	Research has not found a link between blood types and personality.		for	against
5	Statistical data often give evidence for a blood type-personality connection.		for	against
6	Friends often seem to match the blood type-personality categories.		for	against

Grammar Point

強調

1. 助動詞 do を用いた強調：「本当に、確かに」

   *Secondly, there **does** seem to be some statistical evidence for the categories.*

   ▍動詞の前に置いて、文の内容が事実であることを強調する

2. on earth：「一体（全体）～」

   *How **on earth** could that affect personality?*

   ▍疑問詞の直後に用いて疑問詞を強調する

UNIT 17

Writing

次の例文を参考にして、**notice** の使い方を学習しましょう。

「～に気づく」を意味する動詞の notice は、さまざまなテーマについて話し合う際に使われます。

1. Many people **notice** that many of their friends' personalities match blood type-personality categories.

2. Many people **notice** that most of their friends do not match the categories.

「すでに気づいている」ことについて語る時は、次のように現在完了形を使いましょう。

3. I **have noticed** that I exactly match the personality category for my blood type.

4. My brother is blood type B, but I **haven't noticed** that he is active.

それでは、下欄の agree か disagree を○で囲み、動詞の notice を使って空欄を英語で埋めましょう。もし、notice を使って答えるのが難しい場合は、これまでの章で学んだものを使用してください。

I agree / disagree with this proposal.

_____

_____

Listening Dictation

CD を聞いて次の空欄を埋めましょう。

1. My best ¹⁾(　　　　) is blood type A, but I have noticed that her personality is completely ²⁾(　　　　) from other A-type people.

2. If we try to ¹⁾(　　　　) someone's blood type just from their personality, more often than not we will ²⁾(　　　　).

3. Talking about blood types is ¹⁾(　　　　) and also a good way to get to ²⁾(　　　　) people.

Speaking

次の会話モデルを使用して、クラスメートや先生にあなたの意見を伝えてみましょう。また、先ほど学習した表現方法も積極的に使いましょう。

- **A** May I ask a personal question?
- **B** Sure, go ahead.
- **A** What blood type are you?
- **B** I'm blood type _____.
- **A** Really? I'm type _____.
- **B** That's interesting.
- **A** Do you think blood types are useful for categorizing people's personalities?
- **B** That's an interesting question! Well, I guess… yes, I do.   OR   no, I don't.
- **A** Why do you say that?
- **B** [reason] _____
- **A** I see.
- **B** How about you? What do you think?
- **A** Well, I think that, yes, they are / no, they aren't. [reason] _____

　　信じる・信じないにかかわらず、昔から日本人は血液型と性格を結びつけることが好きな国民と言えるかもしれません。そしてそれは、本文でも触れられていましたが、一部の企業の人事にも影響を及ぼすことがあるようです。

　　例えば、ある学生が採用面接の際に血液型を聞かれて「B型です」と答えたら不採用になったり、また、ある企業が商品開発で斬新なアイデアを得るために、AB型の社員ばかりを集めてプロジェクトチームを作ったということがあったそうです。

　　もちろん、血液型だけを理由に不採用にすることは、今では不当だとはっきり認められていますので、安心してください。

UNIT 18 Cosmetic Surgery

まだ日本では美容整形は一般的とは言えませんが、自分がする・しないにかかわらず、美容整形に対してあなたはどのような考えを持っていますか。

Vocabulary in Context

次の空欄に入る語を以下の語群から選んでください。また必要に応じて語の形を変化させましょう。

1. I will finish this job in one week. You have my _____ .
2. Cosmetic surgery will certainly give you a(n) _____ improvement.
3. Do not worry about your _____ . What is inside is more important.
4. The doctor _____ the operation very well.
5. I have a tattoo on my arm but it is usually _____ under my clothes.
6. I suggested cosmetic surgery to my friend but he _____ the idea.

> hide   appearance   perform   reject   physical   guarantee

テーマ 美容整形は良いことである

1 Would you have cosmetic surgery? Perhaps, in Japan, most people will answer "No" to this question. However, if we think about it rationally, cosmetic surgery does in fact have many good points.

2 Firstly and above all, cosmetic surgery is effective. It will make you look better. And the improvement is not something hidden; it is something that you and the people around you will see every day.

3 Secondly, this improvement will have a positive psychological effect. Many people who are unsatisfied with their appearance have low self-esteem and are very shy. Cosmetic surgery will change not only your outer appearance but also the inner you, thus helping to boost your self-confidence.

4 Finally, these days, cosmetic surgery is safe. Medical techniques have improved amazingly in recent years, and there are many excellent cosmetic surgeons who can quickly and safely perform the surgery.

5 Cosmetic surgery may be popular in other countries but here in Japan it has a somewhat negative image. There are several reasons why we should reject cosmetic surgery.

6 Firstly, cosmetic surgery is unnecessary because our outer appearance is just one small part of us. As people say, true beauty comes from within. Thus a good, kind and friendly person is truly beautiful, regardless of looks.

7 Secondly, any kind of surgery has some risks and, without doubt, cosmetic surgery is risky. People have suffered permanent physical damage and pain from botched cosmetic surgery. In the worst cases, people have died. Having unnecessary surgery is simply not worth the risk.

8 Finally, there is no guarantee that the end result will be an improvement. In some cases, people have ended up looking worse than before. Imagine spending all that money on something which, in the end, gives a negative result!

UNIT 18

> **Note**
> **cosmetic surgery** 美容整形　**rationally** 合理的に　**self-esteem** 自尊心　**boost ~** ~を高める　**self-confidence** 自信　**medical technique** 医療技術　**cosmetic surgeon** 美容整形外科医　**somewhat** いくぶん、やや（副詞）　**within** 内面、内側（名詞）　**botched** 失敗した、下手な（botchは「やり損なう、だめにする」の意味）　**the end result** 仕上がり、最終結果（endは形容詞）　**end up ~ing** 最終的には~になる

Comprehension

次の文は本文の内容を要約したものです。該当する段落の番号を空欄に書き入れて、for または against のどちらかを○で囲んでください。

			for/against
1	Inside is most important so cosmetic surgery is not necessary.		for / against
2	There are dangers in getting cosmetic surgery.		for / against
3	The final result might look worse.		for / against
4	Modern surgery is very safe.		for / against
5	Cosmetic surgery will improve your appearance.		for / against
6	Successful surgery will improve your confidence.		for / against

Grammar Point

同格のthat ：「~という…」

*Finally, there is no **guarantee that** the end result will be an improvement.*

> 先行する名詞（*guarantee*）の内容を、それに続くthat節が説明している。また次の例文のように、先行する名詞（*suggestion*）とthat節が離れる場合もある。
>
> 例 The **suggestion** was made **that** language teaching should be improved.

Writing

次の例文を参考にして、形容詞を使った意見の述べ方を学びましょう。

Cosmetic surgery is
- ... effective.
- ... safe.
- ... unnecessary.
- ... risky.

意見を述べる際に形容詞を使うと便利ですが、以下のように、短い説明を加える必要があります。

1. Cosmetic surgery is **effective**. It will improve your appearance.
2. Cosmetic surgery is **dangerous** because the operation might not be successful.

それでは下欄の for か against を○で囲み、上の例文のように、英語でその理由を書いてください。

I am for / against   this proposal.

___

___

Listening Dictation

CD を聞いて次の空欄を埋めましょう。

1. Cosmetic surgery is useful, not only as ¹⁾(   ) treatment. It can also help people who have had an ²⁾(   ), for example.

2. It is often easy to ¹⁾(   ) that somebody has had cosmetic surgery. It looks ²⁾(   ).

3. I wouldn't have ¹⁾(   ) cosmetic surgery but something ²⁾(   ) might be acceptable.

UNIT 18

Speaking

次の会話モデルを使用して、クラスメートや先生にあなたの意見を伝えてみましょう。また、先ほど学習した表現も積極的に使いましょう。

A Do you think that cosmetic surgery is good?

B Hmm. Let me see. Well,… yes, I do.　　OR　　no, I don't.

A OK. Why do you say that?

B [reason] _____

A Any other reasons?

B [reason] _____

A I see. That's interesting.

B How about you? What do you think?

A I (also) think it's good.　OR　I (also) think it's not good.

B Could you explain why?

A Sure. [reason] _____

　　国によって美容整形に対する受け止め方はさまざまですが、美容整形大国のひとつである南米のブラジルでは、驚いたことに、美容整形が人だけではなく、ペットにも広がっているようです。

　　ブラジルでは、愛するペットの見た目を自分好みにするために、飼い主が病院で尻尾を短くしたり耳の形を整えたりするケースが相次いだようで、これを問題視したリオデジャネイロの州議会が、犬と猫への美容整形手術を禁止する法案を2014年に可決したそうです。

UNIT 19 Ear Piercing

男性と女性で意見は大きく異なるかもしれませんが、
あなたはピアスをする人をどう思いますか。
また、自分でもしてみたいと思いますか。

Vocabulary in Context

次の下線部に入る語を以下の語群から選んでください。

1. I try to _____ jewelry containing nickel because I am allergic to it.
2. These gold earrings will _____ a hint of luxury to your look.
3. Do women think that earrings on men look _____?
4. There is _____ that people wore earrings thousands of years ago.
5. Some people have a(n) _____ image of body piercings such as lip rings.
6. According to a survey, the _____ of women wear jewelry every day.

| majority | avoid | negative | evidence | attractive | add |

テーマ　ピアスはするべきでない

For

① Looking at my female university friends, it seems that the majority have their ears pierced. Even many guys have pierced ears these days.

② In my opinion, however, ear piercing is something that we should avoid. I have three reasons for thinking this way.

③ Firstly, the natural and undecorated state is the most beautiful condition for the human body. If you touch a pierced ear, the metal feels harsh and unnatural against the soft skin.

④ Secondly, making an unnatural hole in your body can be bad for your health. One friend of mine got a nasty infection from the pierced hole in her ear. Another friend often gets allergic reactions to the metals used in earrings. They seem to be suffering unnecessarily.

⑤ Thirdly, having unpierced ears makes life easier! You save a little time getting ready in the morning and you can avoid that terrible frustration of always losing one earring of a pair.

Against

⑥ Having pierced ears is a good thing. The fact that the majority of young women have pierced ears is evidence that it is popular and well-accepted.

⑦ There are three main arguments in support of ear piercing.

⑧ Firstly, earrings in pierced ears look very attractive. Whether a cute style or a glamorous one, simple or showy, a beautiful pair of earrings adds the finishing touch to your appearance.

⑨ Secondly, earrings fulfill the natural human urge to decorate things. As humans, we love to decorate our surroundings, our possessions and ourselves. To put it simply, decorating something plain makes it more attractive.

⑩ Finally, earrings can act as a form of communication. When people meet you for the first time, they look for non-verbal cues to learn more about you. Accessories such as earrings can tell people something about your character in a subtle way.

> **Note**
> **undecorated** 装飾していない　**harsh** ゴツゴツした　**nasty infection** ひどい感染症　**allergic reaction** アレルギー反応　**glamorous** 魅惑的な　**showy** 派手な、華やかな　**finishing touch** 最後の仕上げ（touchは「一筆」の意味）　**urge to do** 〜したいという衝動　**to put it simply** 簡単に言えば　**non-verbal cue** 非言語的手がかり（表情やジェスチャーなど）　**in a subtle way** それとなく（subtleは「とらえがたい、微妙な」の意味）

Comprehension

次の文は本文の内容を要約したものです。該当する段落の番号を空欄に書き入れて、for または against のどちらかを○で囲んでください。

①	Earrings give you an opportunity to express something about yourself.		for	against
②	Life is simpler without earrings.		for	against
③	Humans have a tendency to beautify things.		for	against
④	There are some health risks connected with getting your ears pierced.		for	against
⑤	Having pierced ears looks beautiful.		for	against
⑥	The human body is most beautiful without decoration.		for	against

Grammar Point

whether の主な用法

1. whether A or B 「AであろうとBであろうと」
   Whether *a cute style **or** a glamorous one, simple **or** showy, a beautiful pair of earrings adds the finishing touch to your appearance.*
   > 上の文の場合、Whether A or B, C or D「AであろうとBであろうと、CであろうとDであろうと」という意味になる。

2. whether A or B 「AかまたはBか」
   例 I don't know **whether** he is at home **or** at the office.

Writing

次の２つの例文を参考にして、**can** の使い方を学習しましょう。

> can は「〜できる」(能力) のほかに、「〜することがありうる」(可能性) を表すこともあります。

1. I **can** make jewelry. For example, I made this necklace myself.（能力）
2. Anyone **can** make mistakes, especially when you are young.（可能性）

それでは下欄の agree か disagree を○で囲み、どこか１箇所を選んでその理由を英語で書いてみましょう。

I agree / disagree with this proposal.

Having pierced ears can _____

or

Having unpierced ears can _____

or

Earrings can _____

Listening Dictation

CD を聞いて次の空欄を埋めましょう。

1. ¹⁾(　　　　) many years, earrings can pull down on your *earlobes and change their ²⁾(　　　　) .　　　　　　　　　*earlobe：耳たぶ

2. ¹⁾(　　　　) are more types of earrings for pierced ears ²⁾(　　　　) *clip-on earrings.　　　　　　*clip-on earring：クリップ式イヤリング

3. I ¹⁾(　　　　) ²⁾(　　　　) get my ears pierced but my parents won't ³⁾(　　　　) it.

Speaking

次の会話モデルを使用して、クラスメートや先生にあなたの意見を伝えてください。また、先ほど学習した表現も積極的に使いましょう。

A What do you think about having pierced ears? Are you for it or against it?

B Well, I guess that I am _____

A Really? Why is that?

B [reason] _____

A OK. I see. Anything else?

B [reason] _____

A Right. I understand.

B How about you? Are you for it or against it?

A Actually, I think the same as you. *OR*   I am _____

B OK. Could you explain why?

A Sure. [reason] _____

　日本ではピアスに対して賛否両論ありますが、世界の国々は日本とは大いに状況が異なるようです。なんとスペインでは、性別の判断ミスを避ける意味もあって、生後2～3日の間に女の子にピアスの穴を開ける習慣があるそうです。またイランでは、生後6日目に名付け祝いを兼ねて、魔除けの意味でピアスの穴開けが行われるようです。

　赤ちゃんへのピアスなど日本ではとうてい考えられませんが、ちなみに米国のある学会によると、感染症や合併症の予防が適切にできる医師であれば、子どもの耳にピアスの穴を開ける行為は基本的に安全だそうです。

UNIT 20 Wearing Perfume

あるデータによると、日本人の約4人に1人は香水のにおいが苦手のようです。
あなたは、香水に興味がありますか。

Vocabulary in Context

次の空欄に入る語を以下の語群から選んでください。

1. This perfume is safe to spray _____ on your body.
2. It is my _____ to wear perfume every day.
3. My skin is very _____, so I avoid using strong perfumes.
4. There are _____ types of perfume.
5. Not all perfumes are expensive. Some nice ones are _____ cheap.
6. This perfume was a bad _____. It doesn't match my personality.

| relatively | choice | various | directly | custom | sensitive |

香水をつけるのは良いことである

 For

1 Do you wear perfume or cologne? It seems that relatively few people in Japan do so. However, perhaps it is worth thinking again about perfume.

2 Firstly, wearing perfume adds something to your image. For a lady, a good fragrance can make her seem more feminine or more elegant. For a gentleman, a good choice of cologne can give a strong, masculine impression, or else a fresh and clean image.

3 Secondly, wearing perfume is fun. There are so many different types to choose from. Just visiting a department store and smelling the various brands is enjoyable and, if you find a fragrance that you really like, it is a great feeling.

4 Finally, a perfume, cologne or aftershave makes a very nice birthday or Christmas gift. It is personal, not cheap but not too expensive, and the recipient can wear it on the next date!

5 Let's start using perfume more.

 Against

6 When Japanese people travel abroad, one thing they sometimes notice is that foreign people seem to wear perfume more than Japanese people. In my opinion, it is best that Japanese people do not use perfume so much.

7 Firstly, we do not have a tradition of wearing perfume. Although part of Japanese culture is to use flowers or fruit to create a pleasant aroma in a room, spraying perfume directly onto the skin is not our custom.

8 Secondly, wearing fragrance is inconsiderate to other people around us. If we put on perfume, other people on the train or in the office will smell it, whether they want to or not.

9 Finally, many perfumes and colognes have very strong smells. Japanese people seem to be very sensitive to different aromas and, what might be a mild fragrance for people in other countries, may be overpowering for us.

10 Let's refrain from using perfume.

UNIT 20

Note

cologne オーデコロン（香水のひとつ）　**fragrance** 香り　**feminine** 女性らしい　**masculine** 男性らしい　**or else** でなければ、もしくは　**aftershave** アフターシェーブローション（ひげそりの後につける化粧水）　**recipient** 受け取った人　**aroma** 香り　**inconsiderate** 配慮のない　**overpowering** 強烈な

Comprehension

次の文は本文の内容を要約したものです。該当する段落の番号を空欄に書き入れて、for または against のどちらかを○で囲んでください。

①	The smell of many perfumes is too strong.		for	against
②	It is fun to buy and wear perfumes.		for	against
③	It is not fair to other people to wear perfume.		for	against
④	You can enhance your image with a nice perfume.		for	against
⑤	Japanese people do not have the custom to use perfume.		for	against
⑥	A gift of perfume is very nice.		for	against

Grammar Point

関係代名詞の what

「〜すること（もの）」という意味を表し、先行詞なしで使う。whatの導く節は名詞節で、文の主語・目的語・補語になる。

1. 主　語　… **what** might be a mild fragrance for people in other countries, may be overpowering for us.
2. 目的語　I don't believe **what** you are saying.
3. 補　語　The smartphone is just **what** I wanted.

Writing

次の例文を参考にして、if 節の表現を学習しましょう。

1. **If** you **find** a fragrance that you really like, **it** is a great feeling.

   「If + S + 動詞の現在形, S + 動詞の現在形」の形をとります。
   推論ではなく事実を示す場合にこの形が使用され、if = when となります。

2. **If** we **put on** perfume, other people on the train or in the office **will smell** it.

   「If + S + 動詞の現在形, S + will + 動詞の原形」の形をとります。
   あることが起これば、その結果他のことが起こるだろう、という場合に使用されます。

それでは下欄の agree か disagree を○で囲み、上のどちらかの表現を使って空欄を英語で埋めてください。なお、Ifを使って答えるのが難しい場合は、これまでの章で学んだものを使用しましょう。

I agree / disagree with this proposal.

_____

_____

Listening Dictation

CD を聞いて次の空欄を埋めましょう。

1. If you choose a ¹⁾(　　　　) perfume, it will not ²⁾(　　　　) other people.

2. Some people have very ¹⁾(　　　　) skin and may get a *rash if they ²⁾(　　　　) perfume.   *rash:発疹

3. I like wearing perfume but only do so on ¹⁾(　　　　) occasions such as ²⁾(　　　　) .

UNIT 20

Speaking

次の会話モデルを使用して、クラスメートや先生にあなたの意見を伝えてみましょう。また、先ほど学習した表現も積極的に使いましょう。

A Do you think wearing perfume is nice?

B Now, that's an interesting question.
Umm… yes, I do.　OR　no, I don't.

A Really? Why do you say that?

B [reason] _____

A OK. Anything else?

B [reason] _____

A I understand!

B How about you. What do you think?

A I (also) think wearing perfume is good / not so good.

B Please explain.

A Sure. [reason] _____

歴史的に見ると、香水はフランスで発達して世界中に広まったと言われています。16世から17世紀のヨーロッパ、特にフランスでは、お風呂に入ると梅毒などの病気になりやすいと信じられていたため、人々は水に対して恐怖心を抱き、入浴を避けていました。（現在でも「風呂嫌い」のフランス人は多いと言われています。）そのため、体臭を消す必要に迫られて、さまざまな香りの香水が発達したそうです。昔から毎日入浴する習慣のあった日本人の間に、香水があまり普及しなかったのもうなずけます。

TEXT PRODUCTION STAFF

edited by
Eiichi Kanno
Taiichi Sano

編集
菅野 英一
佐野 泰一

English-language editing by
Bill Benfield

英文校閲
ビル・ベンフィールド

cover design by
Ruben Frosali

表紙デザイン
ルーベン・フロサリ

illustrated by
IOK Co., Ltd.

イラスト
株式会社 イオック

CD PRODUCTION STAFF

recorded by
Kimberly Tierney (AmE)
Howard Colefield (AmE)

吹き込み者
キンバリー・ティエニー（アメリカ英語）
ハワード・コールフィールド（アメリカ英語）

Thanks to Hiroaki, Masato, Mariko and Kyoko.

Two Sides to Every Discussion
英語で考え、英語で発信する

2016年1月20日　初版発行
2025年2月25日　第12刷発行

著　者　Jonathan Lynch
　　　　委文 光太郎
発行者　佐野 英一郎
発行所　株式会社 成美堂
　　　　〒101-0052　東京都千代田区神田小川町3-22
　　　　TEL 03-3291-2261　FAX 03-3293-5490
　　　　https://www.seibido.co.jp

印刷・製本　三美印刷(株)

ISBN 978-4-7919-4784-3　　　　　　　　　　Printed in Japan

・落丁・乱丁本はお取り替えします。
・本書の無断複写は、著作権上の例外を除き著作権侵害となります。